THE
Compromising
OF THE
Constitution

THE

Compromising

OF THE

Constitution

(Early Departures)

REXFORD G. TUGWELL

UNIVERSITY OF NOTRE DAME PRESS
NOTRE DAME   LONDON

Library of Congress Cataloging in Publication Data

Tugwell, Rexford Guy, 1891-
    The compromising of the Constitution (early departures).

    1. United States—Constitutional law—Interpretation
and construction.   2. Judicial review—United States.
I. Title.
KF4550.T83   342'.73'03   76-641
ISBN 0-268-00714-4

                Manufactured in the United States of America

Contents

Foreword

This essay is meant to be part of a continuing discussion about the enlarging of the Constitution by implication. The recasting of that document has been (and is being) done by others than *the people* to whom, according to the preamble, it belongs. It does not need to be said that it is a serious matter to change the Constitution and that presumably, since it is the supreme law of the land, it ought to be altered only in a process similar to the original one. It is because this process was made so difficult, and because changes have been urgently required, that they have been made by extension—that is, by assuming that the Constitution's directives imply whatever allowances of power are necessary to what is sought to be done. For instance, it is argued that the Congress cannot legislate without being allowed to investigate or that the president cannot execute the laws without confidential communications; if the Constitution did not specify any such allowances they were nonetheless intended by the Framers. This gives the study of implication its fascination. A useful metaphor might be the escape of the storied genies from their vessels. Once a power has escaped its constitutional confinement it seldom gets put back and it tends to enlarge indefinitely. But, of course, there are several governmental vessels and so several escaped genies. They occupy the same space, sometimes, or try to, and so mingle in confused conflict with each other.

If this seems fanciful, consider the executive and congressional privileges to be examined here: how they are derived, how they are defended, how they frustrate each other. Or, consider the nature and uses of emergency, when Congress and president unite to create an authority completely unknown to the Constitution.

The inquiry required the location of the vessels and seeing, if that was possible, how they were first opened for the genie to escape. The questioning of General St. Clair's defeat was, for instance, the beginning of congressional investigation. It was not begun for any legislative purpose. It was a political impulse to embarrass the Federalists, but it opened the lid and led, after more than a century, to an Un-American Activities Committee and to a controller general. Similarly, the genie inside the vessel of faithful execution of the laws, led in the end to executive budgets and impoundment.

The genies still escape. The Congress, with the excuse of "recovering its powers" after the Nixon expansion, created a budget bureau of its own. It was necessary, it was said, if the exclusive power to lay taxes was to have a proper definition of the amount needed. Actually, it was more than that. It was intended to gain more control of executive processes in contravention of any possible constitutional warrant. The president began to extend his own "privilege" to all members of his administration, to impound such authorized funds as he disapproved; and even, sometimes, to invent powers that did not exist.

Interpretation and extrapolation have gone so far, in some instances, that relation to any original constitutional directive is remote or nonexistent. When this has occurred, legitimacy has, in fact, been abandoned. This conclusion is rejected by those who, for one reason or another, find clarity inconvenient and desire to impose their own interpretation on ambiguous clauses. This was foreseen by certain of the Framers, among them Hamilton and Madison, to whom reference will be made. They regarded the possibility of differing interpretations in opposing ways and their views were the beginning of controversies that have persisted ever since. Those early differences are discussed in what follows. Advocates of loose and strict construction were at odds even in Washington's time.

It is one of the curiosities of our history that not one of these disagreements has ever been put to rest by amendment. They have remained in a kind of limbo. Each branch, each agency, each official has claimed powers not to be found in the Constitution and they have never been given up except in grudging and unacknowledged compromise. When this happens the issues retreat into shadows whence they emerge on subsequent occasions with the same accompaniment of argumentative paraphernalia.

Why this network of illegitimacy developed, it was thought, might be somewhat clarified by the identification of departure points and the justifications offered by the then contemporaries.

Acknowledgment

Acknowledgment is gratefully made of critical appraisal by colleagues at the Center for the Study of Democratic Institutions, for special assistance by Richard Kipling and for advice from Louis Fisher of the Congressional Research Service. I am indebted also to my former colleague at Chicago, C. H. Pritchett, whose texts are rich sources of constitutional meanings and to Theodore Lowi for calling my attention to the relevance of Carl Becker's essay on the Constitution. Any acknowledgment, however, would be incomplete without referring to Leo S. Rowe, who taught my first course in constitutional law at the University of Pennsylvania and afterward went on to give the Pan American Union its valuable position among international organizations.

1: Definition

Direct and explicit definition is hard to find among the early American political writers who had a part in, or who influenced those who had a part in, the making of the Constitution in 1787. When Hamilton and Madison, with Jay, collaborated in writing *The Federalist* under the pseudonym of Publius, they did speak for those who had prevailed at the convention; but they apparently felt no need to explain how the constitutional government they had created differed from other kinds except to point out that it alone was owed to the people. Many historical examples were used, but always with some relation to the convention's completed work, and mostly the ones they used were deplored.

The learning of such delegates as Madison, Morris, Wilson and Mason was certainly extensive; but their use of it in designing the Constitution's provisions was meagre. They were engaged in a practical task and went about it earnestly but with few preconceptions. There were no national models and their borrowings were from the immediate past, especially the legal systems and governments they were familiar with, mostly, of course, the British. They relied on their own experience and their conception of the nation's necessities.

They were concerned about their own interests and those of their close countrymen, but most of all with the union they were creating out of disparate elements. Sectionalism was far sharper than is easily understood by later generations, and finding accommodation was a frequent necessity among the delegates. There was fear that any central government would be controlled by New England, say, or the South, and would be injurious to the enterprises of other regions. One proposal, considered momentarily, was for three executives, one for each section of the country. Such an arrangement might have appeased sectional advocates but would have made genuine union impossible, and common sense prevailed.

The search for union acceptable to reluctant state politicians was another practical difficulty, but once sovereignty and tripartite powers were agreed to the rest was not so difficult.

Hamilton did venture the generalization at the ratification convention that "good constitutions are formed upon a comparison of the liberty of the individual with the strength of government"; and he explained further:

> ... if the tone of either be too high, the other will be weakened too much. It is the happiest possible mode of conciliating these objects to institute one branch peculiarly endowed with sensibility, another with knowledge and firmness. Through the opposition and control of these bodies, the government will reach, in its operations, the perfect balance between liberty and power.

This, however, was less a reflection on the nature, or even the uses, of constitutions than a comment on the necessity for separated but interacting branches as a structural frame. Hamilton, like Madison and Jay, and like the convention's majority, argued that such an arrangement would secure both individual rights and national unity. Because of the existing government's fatal weakness he had for a long time been urging the necessity for stronger union.* The Constitution, he argued, would provide what had until then been lacking. Behind this, however, there was certainly some such feeling as was detected by historian Carl Becker, concerning the character of the compact. In that revolutionary age, man's simple allotted task was to create a constitution that would "bring his ideas, his actions and his institutions into harmony with the universal laws of nature...."

> Since social evils are the results of ignorance or neglect of the natural rights of man, the first task of political science is to define these rights, the second to devise a mechanism of government suited to guarantee them.

The devising of such an instrument could be the work of weeks rather than years because

> ... its principles were the result of a century of enlightenment, and little more was required than to transcribe on the tablets of the law the eternal truths engraved on the hearts of all men. ...**

Nevertheless, it must be regarded as remarkable that so great a work could be completed in one uncomfortable Philadelphia summer. The accomplishment is indeed accountable only by realizing that there were accepted principles: the delegates had no need to argue again the great questions of governance. Political philosophy had been under discussion in America for at least

*As Rossiter has shown in *Alexander Hamilton and the Constitution, 1780–1788* (New York: Harcourt, Brace & World, 1964).
**Carl L. Becker, "Afterthoughts on Constitutions" in *The Constitution Reconsidered*, ed. Conyers Read (New York: Columbia University Press, 1938).

a hundred years, one result being the drafting by Jefferson of the Declaration of Independence, but such eloquent formulations could give way in Philadelphia to discussions mostly about ways to achieve union without too much sacrifice of the states' interests or individual liberties. The delegates bargained about these matters and reached compromises; what emerged was a charter none of them approved in every part but most—not all—felt was good enough to go on with until experience had shown what changes were needed.* None could have expected or wanted it to endure intact for very long, but it did have a core of consent to government with more powers than had been conceded to the languishing Continental Congress. It did, for instance, provide for a national sphere of sovereignty with a separately elected executive.

Whatever their particular provisions, such constitutions are at once a formulation of principles and a structure for government. They assign powers and guard against their abuse. They enumerate rights but curb excesses. They are citizens' compacts with each other, composed by specially chosen delegates and ratified by their representatives. The first words of this one, "We, the people" were an intended reference and were sufficiently exact.** It has also to be kept in mind that such constitutions, when ratified, are the highest law of na-

---

*Such delegates as Randolph and Mason, having participated throughout, finally refused to sign; certain others, such as Yates and Lansing had departed as soon as they understood what way the deliberations were likely to go.

**Although the antifederalists would have substituted, as Patrick Henry demanded, "We, the States." It should also be recalled that by "people" the Framers meant those who were white, male, and possessors of property. This was probably not more than 10 percent of the adult population.

tions, above and beyond ordinary rules of conduct and definitions of mutual relations. More significant, they are anterior to, and a framework for, legislated acts. They represent better than anything else the national spirit and are the symbol of its intentions. When American officials are inaugurated they swear to "preserve, protect, and defend" not the government but the Constitution.

One unfortunate consequence of this is that the respect constitutions command tends to become exaggerated and even irrational. The virtues, the situations, and the relations they assume, accepted when written, continue into other and changed times and so they tend to become irrelevant. To avoid this they must be brief and general; if they are lengthy or overspecific they risk obsolescence, perhaps soon. Brief and general statements, however, are ambiguous and so subject to interpretation, and interpretations accord with opinion, prejudice, and difference of view about what was originally intended or is presently wise.

It is accurate to call decisions of the Supreme Court justices, who are entrusted with this task, "opinions." They seem to have a coloration of finality; nevertheless, the last word, as the authors of *The Federalist* observed, is the prerogative of the people. As will be seen, however, immense and unnecessary difficulties were imposed on the exercising of this peoples' prerogative. The power is there to be summoned when needed, but the need must be overwhelming, a last resort when all else has failed, and even then will be disputed among seekers for advantage.

The American Constitution was devised for a republic not yet democratized—wherefrom much of its elitist quality. Nevertheless it provided a system of government. Other organizations of people often give the same name to documents; but these have no such place in the national esteem. Even the American version's faults are peculiar ones. The agreement it represents is one that was reached in an unusually troubled time. A rebellion was in process of being consolidated after years of foreign rule and a protracted war. The circumscribing of governmental powers was at least as prominent in the Framers' minds as the structuring of a serviceable organization. This is why there are so many prohibitions and so few instructions. Most of what government may *not* do is stated clearly, but what it *must* do is mostly implied. Protections for certain interests are specified; so are prohibitions of abuses; but duties and responsibilities often have to be guessed at. Hamilton, in *The Federalist,* spoke repeatedly and enthusiastically of the energies the Constitution would release, but actually it had more curbs on initiative than encouragements to act. Obviously it was not expected that the responsibilities of the national government would be extensive or that citizens would be expected to give it more than nominal recognition. The states were still fully operative.

The Constitution, being sufficient for its time, but not having been changed substantially for nearly two centuries, has, to put it plainly, become in many respects obsolete. The succeeding generations still living within its directives are confronted with conditions radically different from those known to the original framers. The arguments it emerged from are no longer relevant and its governance of the nation has become more mystical than real.

Such of its provisions as have become hopelessly outdated—that is, if those provisions are taken literally—

must be cast in one way or another, and, of course, the casting goes on all the time. In this process the attribution to "the people" becomes attenuated. Does anyone believe that if the Constitution in its entirety should be submitted to referendum now, and relieved somehow of its traditional sanctity, it would be ratified? If it would not, and if constitutional government is desirable, then it follows that an acceptable one ought to be devised. This simple logic seems irrefutable; actually it is universally evaded. It is even widely regarded as reprehensible to make such a suggestion.

It is contended by those who are by temperament or from interest opposed to change that the original draft expressed enduring principles as valid at one time as at any other. If the analogy is allowable, something of the sort is also said when the Ten Commandments are defended by the orthodox. About these it could be remarked that the coveting of asses is no longer a frequent temptation, and that there is a certain erosion of credibility about any such formulation. Of the Bill of Rights it can equally be said that the quartering of soldiers in people's houses is no longer a useful prohibition, that "a well-regulated militia" is a poor excuse for possession by citizens of millions of lethal weapons, and that twenty dollars is hardly a practical dividing line between disputes requiring trial by jury and those not requiring one. The Commandments are the concern of religious leaders, but the provisions of the Constitution are presumed to be enforceable injunctions.

The clause about the quartering of soldiers can be disregarded as simply emptied of meaning, but the bearing of arms and the twenty dollars clause remain as embarrassing anachronisms. This, without much reflection, may be said about some more consequential provisions. The terms stated for president and legislators may have been well suited to the conditions of the 1780's, when the election of selectmen was the prevailing model. These terms, however, are not so well suited to the executive and legislative needs of a continental electorate. "Checks and balances" were intended to prevent the lodging of absolute authority anywhere, but some of them may make it difficult or impossible to move when newly arising problems must be solved. A second legislative house with malapportioned representation may have conciliated antiunionist politicians at the Convention, but the awkward compromise need not have been retained into an indefinite future. The Senate, as now constituted, is an indefensible survivor.

Those who are seriously hampered by constitutional anachronisms have legitimate complaints. Where in the Constitution is it said that education, health, or the conspicuous ills of industrial society may be in any way reached by governmental action? Or for that matter, the controlling of economic conditions? Only by implication can such activities be justified, and the implication, as we shall see, is sometimes remote from its source and subject to varieties of interpretation. Consequently, no one knows what may or may not be done when action becomes imperative.

The difficulty is made worse by uncertainty whether national powers were meant to include only those specifically listed in the Constitution. It was the theory of federalism that all those powers not specified as belonging to the central government would belong to the states. As everyone knows, however, there has been a continued attenuation of local prerogatives and an accompanying expansion of the national reach. It has, for instance, required many years and numerous court opinions to settle on meanings for the power to regulate commerce among the states. As a result of slow attrition very little commerce has been left for the states to regulate, but just how much no one can be certain. Final definitions have never been made. This is one example of the many long and involved disputes about interpretation suffered by all those whose affairs are in any way involved in the ambiguities made inevitable by compromise at the Convention and by the brevity and generality of the final draft by the committee on style. Most such difficulties are amenable enough to clearing up; only a few phrases would suffice; but they would have to be incorporated in the Constitution itself.

A constitution does contain specifications for the devices of government as well as a careful statement of agreed precepts but the devices lose their usefulness and the precepts do not. The two ought not to be confused. Yet this is what has happened in the American instance, and the efforts made to clarify the issues clouded by this confusion have been wholly ineffective. We shall see why.

It is certainly important that some liberties shall be protected as they were meant to be by the Bill of Rights. Among these are freedom of expression, the presumption of innocence for those accused until they are found guilty, and the prohibition of searches and seizures without probable cause. But to preserve intact the bargains struck at the Convention between political disputants—satisfactory to no one even then—reduces the effectiveness of government. That they should be regarded as permanent and untouchable arrangements does confuse precepts with deals made in a time long past concerning issues no longer visible. Deals will doubtless continue to be made, but at least they should concern contemporary issues.

It is not desirable that election to the House of

Representatives shall continue to be controlled by state politicians, but it is important that bills of attainder shall be prohibited. The privilege awarded the Senate of confirming—or not confirming—presidential appointments is only one balancing mechanism that might give way to some other, but keeping for elected representatives the power to lay taxes is, in contrast, extremely important in a democracy.

If the uses of constitutions in democratic republics is understood, it should be obvious that their directives and prohibitions should be relevant to contemporary circumstances. If they are actually—and not just theoretically—instruments of the people, they must have been accepted in some popular process, and that process should not have been long past. Jefferson remarked in 1803:

> Let us go on perfecting the constitution by adding, by way of amendment, those forms which time and trial show are still wanting.

Concerning this perfection by amendment there was an interesting difference between Jefferson and Hamilton who, as we shall see, consistently argued for free interpretation rather than amendment. This position was that anything the government was given power to do, it could create and use the means for doing, whether or not specific authorization could be found in the Constitution. Jefferson, on the contrary, argued that the powers granted were specific and that any extension or enlargement would require amendment. That this was a difference with serious consequences no one familiar with American history can doubt; it made its appearance in the first administration and continued to appear in later ones. Even as late as the twentieth century there were both Hamiltonians and Jeffersonians waging verbal war on each other with the same arguments the originals were using in the eighteenth century when they sat across from each other at Washington's table.

There had, of course, been a revolutionary change What had been an elitist republic had been transformed by Jeffersonians and Jacksonians into a democratic one. Many of the dissensions carrying over after this transformation were owed to the continued existence of an unchanged Constitution intended for predemocratic times when only substantial property owners could vote and even legislatures were made up of those who were called by Hamilton the rich and wellborn.

As the result of changed circumstances and their interpretation of need, the Supreme Court has added several rights to the original ten. These are: association, movement, privacy, voting, and perhaps education. When the Constitution is altered in this way the effect is quite different from forthright amendment. We shall see that this is so.

2: A Familiar Device

State constitutions written in the years of rebellion were more declarations of independence than genuine constitutions. In fact, several were adopted in 1776 or the years just following. This was true of those for Pennsylvania, Maryland, Delaware, New Jersey, North and South Carolina, and Virginia. Those for New York, Massachusetts, New Hampshire, and Georgia had been in existence for some time.* It is apparent that they were already familiar to most of the delegates when they met in Philadelphia, but what the purpose of these charters was and what arrangements they meant to provide for cannot have been agreed on. They were a relatively new device developed out of unrest and a growing conviction that men possessed natural rights that no government might violate. They owed something to the enlightenment in France, something to philosophers—Montesquieu and Locke, most obviously—but more to the need for stating the alternative to colonialism. Even that of New York, the most relevant, was hardly a model for the document produced by the Framers. The states' libertarian pronouncements were not precepts for governance. Bold as they were in proclaiming indepen-

*F. N. Thorpe, *American Charters, Constitutions and Organic Laws, 1492–1908*, 7 vols. (Washington, D.C.: Government Printing Office, 1909).

dence and liberty, they can have offered no assistance in meeting such issues confronting the delegates at Philadelphia as concurrent sovereignty for states and the nation. Even the system of separate branches with intricate mutual checks was quite different from that of the state constitutions. In what is of most interest here however—provisions for amendment if that should become necessary—some could have given useful leads.

A few recognized the need for reexamination at stated periods; in others this was left to initiation by petition; but most of those making any mention of amendment left initiative to the legislatures. That of Pennsylvania had a more interesting provision. This was a council of censors to be elected every seven years and having responsibility for calling conventions if defective articles should have been discovered, or of making additions "conducive to preserving the rights of the people." It was stipulated that alterations proposed by the censors must be placed in public view at least six months prior to conventions so that the people might have "an opportunity of instructing their delegates on the subject." This council was quite outside the operating system of government. None of the states' organs would have anything to do with revision. The example of Pennsylvania was followed by Vermont in 1777, but no other state had any such arrangement except New York, whose constitution (of 1777) had an article providing for a Council of Revision made up of the governor, the chancellor, and judges of the State Supreme Court. This council was to review all bills and veto those it held to be unconstitutional.

It has to be noted about Pennsylvania's censors that Madison expressed disapproval in *The Federalist* (No. 50); his criticism, however, was centered on membership. The council, he said, being made up of former executives or legislators "was split into two fixed and violent parties." Because of this, *"passion,* not *reason,* must have presided over their deliberations." Other than this, Madison's objections centered on demonstrating that no external arrangements would suffice to maintain separated powers in proper balance. In his opinion only internal ones would do.

Certain delegates at the Convention tried to have adopted some such scheme as that of New York, with a review of legislation that did not depend on external intrusions. It was put forward by Madison himself (on June 6) but without success. After its rejection there was a suggestion that the Supreme Court might have joint revisionary power with the president; either could object, and if either did object the bill would have to be repassed by a two-thirds majority; if both objected the bill would require a three-quarters majority to pass. This proposal was defeated on August 15 and no further effort was made to devise a procedure for the rejection of legislation other than by presidential veto. And there was none for revision from outside the existing government.

When Washington took office and administration was begun in 1789, the Constitution had the provisions for amendment we know of, both initiation and ratification being entrusted to the legislative branches of the federal and state governments acting together. From these arrangements, one originating in the states and one in the Congress, both the executive and the judiciary were excluded. Also there was no recourse to popular approval—no referendum. This was only one of the compromises reached by the delegates when disputes threatened disruption of the Convention; some of these were

to have serious consequences that cannot have been
foreseen.

One disagreement preempted so much time and attention that others were settled with much less consideration. This was the difference between the nationalists,
who wanted a strong central government, and the localists, who wanted to perpetuate the powers of the states.
This conflict was compromised but not solved; it
evolved, in spite of Washington's efforts, into political
parties with continuing differences—Jefferson again being on one side and Hamilton on the other. About this,
Jefferson, of course, prevailed in the sense that he won
the presidency in 1800, but Hamilton had the best of
the struggle in the long run, and in a curious way. When
John Adams, in his last days as president, appointed
John Marshall to be Chief Justice, and Marshall, setting
himself to oppose Jefferson, asserted the Court's right
to say what the Constitution meant, the extension of its
meanings became the prerogative of Hamilton's successors, and these successors were nationalists.

The Court was supposedly one among three branches,
but the powers of the other branches were made subject
to Court determination. Separation in this respect was
made less actual than the original theory had meant it to
be or than the Framers had intended. It is to be noted
also that "we, the people" thus became an attenuated
assertion. "We, the justices" would have been a more
realistic rubric after Marshall handed down his decision
in *Marbury* vs. *Madison* in 1803.

Some of the Framers understood that a Constitution
shaped in one summer would not be suitable for long,
but to have foreseen how drastically it would need to be
altered for future generations would have been too
much to expect. And during the controversies at the

Convention they could hardly have kept in mind at all times the nature and uses of the charter they were creating. They must have been too intent on pushing their convictions as well as their interests to consider the larger and longer consequences of their work. One good illustration of this willingness to sacrifice the future for the present is furnished by what is called by historians "the great compromise" of July. This resolved the impasse reached in the confrontation of the nationalists and the localists. The solution centered on the establishment of a senate with equal representation for both large and small states. That this was a flagrant instance of malapportionment, and so a repudiation of the first principle of representation was ignored in the relief of having found a way of going on with what the delegates had set out to do.

It would be interesting if remarks made by Madison, for instance, or James Wilson, at the beginning of the convention had been recorded. Instead, a resolution of strict secrecy was taken at once. Only such notes as Madison made are of much use, and these are not helpful in trying to discover whether the participants had more in mind than establishing a practical government to replace the dying Congress. Some of them were seriously concerned that "We, the people" should not be an empty phrase and that this should include participation in such changes as might prove necessary in the future. One of these was James Wilson whose influence is known to have been considerable. He seems at least to have been more active in debate than most of the others, and there does exist the text of a lecture he made at the College of Philadelphia some years later (in 1791). He stated then a position he may well have spoken for during the Convention:

By the term constitution, I mean that supreme law, made or ratified by those in whom the sovereign power of the state resides, which prescribes the manner, according to which the state wills that the government should be instituted and administered. From this constitution the government derives its power: by this constitution the power of government must be directed and controlled: of this constitution no alteration can be made by the government; because such an alteration would destroy the foundation of its own authority.

As to the people, however, in whom the sovereign power resides, the case is widely different, and stands upon widely different principles. From their authority the constitution originates: for their safety and felicity it is established: in their hands it is as clay in the hands of the potter: they have the right to mould, to preserve, to improve, to refine, and to finish it as they please. If so; can it be doubted that they have the right likewise to change it? A majority of the society is sufficient for this purpose; and if there be nothing in the change, which can be considered as contrary to the act of original association, or to the intention of those who united under it; all are bound to conform to the resolution of the majority. If the act of original association be infringed, or the intention of those who united under it be violated; the minority are still obliged to suffer the majority to do as they think proper; but are not obliged to submit to the new government. They have a right to retire, to sell their lands, and to carry off their effects.

This could well be taken as an adequate definition of constitutionalism: it identified the origin, the coverage, and the only source of revision. Also it recognized majority rule as a principle and allowed the minority only the privilege of retiring. No other procedure had been discovered since, if union, efficiency, and permanency are regarded as essential.

Many among the delegates must have shared Wilson's views. It is curious, however, that if they did they should have agreed to an amending clause without any provision for referenda, allowing the process to be kept within government, and, moreover, within that branch they most distrusted. The source of democratic power was ignored.

Jefferson, of course, had been in France and had not participated in the proceedings, but through his regular correspondence with Madison he had been influential in establishing principles. Because of this and because of his later prominence in the government, a letter written in retirement (in 1833), when he had experienced the nearly immovable obstacles to amendment, is revealing:

> The states are now so numerous that I despair of ever seeing another amendment to the constitution, although the innovations of time will certainly call, and now already call, for some.

He was right. From 1804 until after the Civil War there were no amendments and then only ones intended to ensure the rights of former slaves, and certainly not ones changing the amending clause so that others than legislators would be admitted to the process.

3: A Block

In any operating system an area of rigidity will force the rest of the organization to regard the blockage as an alarming problem because of its effect on the whole. If the strangulation threatens to interfere with operations, something must be done to eliminate the cause. The need for this will appear even before results begin to be felt, but something like an impending breakdown may be required to overcome the opposition of those with an interest in the existing arrangement. Such blockages may result from a change in circumstances, or, what is even more likely, some alteration may promise improvement. Resistance is likely to continue as it is inserted into the progression. In the end, however, the integrity of the system will be restored or it will fall into disuse.

Automation in manufacture offers a simple illustration: in such a system a series will have been established, one unit feeding into a successor and so on through a progression. A new material may appear or a new process may be suggested and arguments for adoption offered. The novelty may not be an alternate material—plastic rather than wood, aluminum rather than steel, one alloy rather than another—or even a redesigned machine. It may be something insubstantial—a suggestion, an idea, a calculation. It may result from reflection or research rather than from the unexpected appearance of some new thing. In manufacture there are, in fact, constant new offerings of various kinds, and evaluation of their possible contribution is a regular task of management. Substitutions are expected events. Absorption of invention is accepted as something expected and adaptation to it is allowed for. Systems with such capability will constantly renew their effectiveness.

There is obviously a significant difference between the most carefully devised mechanical operation and biological functioning. Inert contrivances can only be changed from without; a living individual, in contrast, possesses internal organs of adjustment. There is a scale among these, of course, but since humans generally possess responsive capabilities, located in various strategic areas, and directed by the most complicated of all known centers—the brain, with its network of communications—the analogy with mechanical systems is suggestive even if it has to be used with caution.

Beyond this biological entity—to use an equally useful analogy—there is another, even more wonderfully conceived. This is society. The survival of individuals was made possible by the forming of groups, but the success of groups was conditioned by their ability to adapt and absorb. There was a certain similarity in this to the principle of outside management in mechanical activity. Factories and other such organizations depend on manipulation for the changes necessary to keep them in working condition and responsive to the demands made on them. Since they possess none of the internal organs necessary to adjustment and no center of direction, changes must be imposed from without if they are to be made at all. Groups are also dependent on external management. The requirement is that they shall discover among their constituent individuals those who can devise and operate controls similar in effect to those of biological organisms. There must be alertness to environmental change, sensitivity to the necessity for adaptation, quickness to grasp possibilities, and a capability of setting in motion the required processes; also the directive center must be capable of commanding the assistance of members with appropriate skills.

It can be seen that during the long shaping of his intelligence it must first have been necessary for man to behave as an individual, regarding externalities as potentially dangerous but possibly useful. Later, when groups and then groups of groups were formed, survival and prospering must have depended on cooperation, on interpersonal communication and leaders' directives, and they must have overcome stubborn resistances, stifled competitiveness, and opposed propensities for aggressiveness and violence.

Since it is the nature of nature that evolution proceeds by the tentative trying of devices or arrangements, and since some prove useful and some do not, many are simply discarded and allowed to disappear. This is a ruthless and unforgiving process. For its operation it is necessary for individuals to live for a while, then die; for groups to develop, then vanish; and the same is true of societies.

Individuals were provided with the means to reach the limit of their intended lives if they proved clever enough and had sufficient self-control to behave in adaptive ways. Groups, being nature's extension of individual life, have no such appointed end, no inevitable death. They may go on indefinitely if given the capacity for survival. It is quite possible for them to be immortal, but the condition for continuance is the devising of an intelligence center with communications and directive mechanisms analogous to those of biological organisms. Lacking it they disappear.

With what appears to be a kind of dim apprehension

of nature's intention, men, having assembled in groups, join them together and establish various kinds of governance. When these have the capability of managing their environment and making arrangements with other groups for existing without resorting to mutual extinction, they survive for as long as they behave appropriately. They have varied kinds of existence; some spread into others' territories, often they become part of one another; but many fail and vanish.

In the past these have been called nations, empires, confederacies, and other names. The most successful and long-lived have established central controls, in various forms and with various contrivances, for the administering of increasingly distant and varied peoples. Others have had short existences because they lacked this capability. During this social evolution, countless generations of individuals continued to exist separately or in small groups and went on contriving. This contriving created a continually changing situation, and the most successful societies encouraged and used whatever resources of ingenuity they developed for extending central management. Some expanded; some disappeared.

If this obvious and elementary statement is allowable, perhaps another may be ventured. It has to do with the state of the world and particularly that part of it under British sovereignty in the eighteenth century.

The British were attempting what the Romans had preceded them in doing and had succeeded in going on with for several centuries; that is, extending their empire indefinitely, and particularly to those parts of the world with resources worth exploiting. By the late eighteenth century the British imperial center was being managed by a curious amalgam of businessmen and aristocrats,

each infusing and reinforcing the other. This elite, however, had become exclusive and ingrowing, and it lacked
what the Romans had once had and then lost—tough
and loyal legions under discipline, with a head reinforced by a widely accepted religious establishment. The
British elite had a state religion, but their king was no
longer a credible deity, and his legions were neither
tough nor well commanded. Many were mercenaries in
the pay of a corrupt and inefficient bureaucracy. The
central governance was sufficiently suited to such far
places as India and other societies willing to remain
passive under a civilian management backed by a meagre
showing of military ceremonial, but they were not at all
suited to America where the population consisted of
British emigres who meant to do some exploiting of
their own. A good many of them regarded the pomposi-
ties of the alien royal governors with resentment. This
was strong enough to sustain a successful rebellion.

For at least a hundred years before the Declaration of
Independence this resentment had been intensifying. It
was added to by the increasing numbers of those in the
new world who regarded themselves as members of a
ruling class with qualifications quite adequate for governing. There were merchants in Boston, New York, and
Philadelphia with ambitions to rival their counterparts
in London; there were also owners of numerous ships at
sea; and there were plantation proprietors whose style
was quite as opulent as that of the English country
gentlemen. Many saw no reason for accepting the rule of
appointed governors from overseas or decrees whose
intent was to suppress their commerce so that British
traders could profit.

Washington and his colleagues demonstrated the folly
of hiring Hessians to suppress Americans who were

exasperated by repeated affronts, and when eventually—in 1787—delegates from the various states gathered under Washington's chairmanship to "perfect" a Union of their own, it was a company with moral and intellectual qualities greatly in contrast with the coterie in London whose members had overreached their capabilities.

The Americans had by then won their independence from overseas control, but not feeling any considerable identity as Americans, even though they spoke of themselves as the United States of America, they had set up, some years before, a loose federation to carry on such limited central activities as they grudgingly thought were needed. These were insufficient for the protection of their borders and even for the regulation of commerce among themselves. Still, there were common colonial resentments, reaching back a long way, and there were some who could see that nationhood was vital if succumbing again to foreign absorption was to be avoided. These nationalists, when the Constitutional Convention met, were forced to compromise with those who equated states' rights with the refusal to accept foreign governance. A national union seemed to states' righters little different from empire, but men of prestige and prominence, being largely unionists, were convinced that there were dangers in the separateness represented by the local politicians. For the moment they prevailed; but they made many compromises they knew to be unwise.

It is more than likely that neither George III nor Lord North had ever heard of Locke, Montesquieu, or even Adam Smith. There were at least a dozen of the delegates at Philadelphia who had, and there were a few who had reached conclusions. It was they who supported the formative ideas embodied at the outset in the Virginia Resolutions.

Among the structural devices accepted after discussion was the basic one of three branches, separated but interlocked. This was not so much owed to theorists such as Montesquieu as to dismal experience with the fading Congress. The need for a central authority had been increasingly obvious for some time.* From this agreement there followed such specification about duties and limitations as could be agreed on. Legislatures were familiar; they had existed even in colonial days, although they had had no more leeway than British governors could be compelled to allow. Since these bodies had been centers of resistance they had a traditional prestige with those who recalled the incidents of rebellion. Not only that, they went far back into English history as opponents of absolutism. It was inevitable that of the three branches the legislative should have the premier place. An executive carried at least some suspicious resemblance to a monarch. Even when it had been accepted that there must be one, arguments went on about its nature—how it could be made effective without being arbitrary. It was a novelty, but contemporary governmental impotence had demonstrated the need for just such a device.

Besides the legislature and the executive, there was the judiciary. This too was a familiar institution. It was, however, very little discussed. Its designated position was apparently assumed to be the traditional one of English courts. It was to preside over the limited num-

*For an account of this development see Louis Fisher, *President and Congress* (New York: Free Press, 1972), pp. 1–14.

ber of cases arising under the new Constitution. Most
litigation would still be within the states; most of it
would be private; and it would arise from adversary
actions. There was no thought of intervention in disputes between the legislature and the executive.

It is still more important to note here that the legislature was allowed powers greater than those of either
executive or judiciary. There was also less difficulty in
specifying a list of its duties and powers than in making
such a list for the presidency.

The nationalists at the Convention did not share the
popular assessments of legislatures. Such assemblies,
they thought, were likely to be too much influenced by
demogogues and consequently to be dangerously radical. This propensity had recently been demonstrated by
the rebellion in Massachusetts led by Daniel Shays. The
demand for repudiated debts and cheapened money had
frightened creditors and men of property generally. The
nationalists, indeed, would have preferred to allow the
president an absolute rejection of congressional acts, but
they had to accept the override (by a two-thirds vote) of
his veto. This was insisted on by those who regarded
representatives as guardians of those with smaller interests. In other ways the nationalists were forced to allow
the legislature more powers than they considered wise.
The president, for instance, could be removed by the
legislature, not by the voters who had elected him; the
laying of taxes was exclusively assigned to the lower
house; and the Senate must confirm all important presidential appointments and agree to any treaties he might
negotiate. None of these concessions, however, was
more important than the arrangement finally arrived at
for amendment.

What the nationalists anticipated concerning future

changes in the Constitution we do not know. Not much about the matter appears in surviving notes. If the amending clause was appended to the document by the committee on style without some expressed doubts, it seems a strange oversight. Gouverneur Morris, chairman of the committee, might have been expected to be well aware that changes would be needed, and soon. All the nationalists, for their own reasons—and many of the states' righters for very different ones—had reservations concerning the final draft. Since there had been many compromises, there must have been those who hoped that it would be amended in the future to make it more conformable to the interests they represented.

What is important about the method adopted, for the purpose here, is that legislatures were allowed—in initiating and in ratifying—to have complete control of the process. The president and the judiciary were excluded. Referendum by conventions was only to be at congressional direction, and such a direction was quite unlikely. Since it is not to be supposed that the intention was to make alterations impossible, it is relevant to ask why, without meaning to, the Framers came very close to doing just that. At least they made any amendment impossible that would affect the prerogatives of legislators. It could have been carelessness, of course, natural in the last days of a difficult meeting; or it could have been acceptance of something familiar and, on the whole, approved. This last seems more likely because legislatures had so often resisted British rule, although the nationalists were wary of their tendency to impulsiveness, the process provided would at least ensure protracted deliberation.

Whatever the reason, the legislative branch was given both initiating and ratifying powers, and the result was what might have been expected. That branch, needing reform most, was made immune to it and became the rigid block in the American system. With every passing decade the Constitution would become more obsolete, and the hardening, begun at the outset, would, as time passed, become more and more impermeable.

The Framers understood that they were creating a system with almost mechanical arrangements—Newtonian, Woodrow Wilson would call it. So far as they could, they protected it from fallible and dishonest officials. Without such a containing system, even able and honest ones would tend to act against one another and waste their energies. They must operate in agreed ways or motion would be overcome by frictions. This system they called a Union.

One reason for agreeing to differently based branches was to keep each of them from acquiring too much power—enough to threaten individual liberties. This, however, so far as the nationalists were concerned, must be thought of as a subsidiary intention. Their main thrust was toward a firm central government to succeed the feeble Confederation. True, it was to leave large areas of action to the states, but it was empowered to reach individual citizens through taxation and could use those taxes for national purposes. It was to be competent for dealing with foreign nations, for controlling commerce among the states and for establishing and maintaining communications. The attempt to limit the powers of such a government by application of the federal principle was not so successful as its proponents would have liked, and this later caused a protracted struggle, but the national energy spoken of so often in *The Federalist,* hampered continually as it was by the localists' dissent, did grow stronger through the following decades.

If, however, the national scope enlarged, the source of its enlargement was not the legislative branch. That was the blocking area in the system, and because it controlled the openings to amendment and had no sense of constitutional integrity it allowed illegitimate seizures of power and progressive distortions of original intention.

A Newtonian system presumes that not only routine operations will proceed smoothly but that adjustments to circumstances will occur when they become necessary. The amending clause was inconsistent with the Framers' idea. Its effect was to prevent changes in the original provisions. When these provisions became impossibly restrictive and ways had to be found to keep the system in some sort of operation, the Constitution tended to be compromised. Its attributions were expanded beyond original intentions, or, in matters not foreseen by the Framers, were simply ignored. Its authority as the governing higher law was attenuated and made uncertain. It was indeed on the way to being lost.

4: Escape from the Block
(Implication)

The accommodation of its higher law to inevitably changing circumstances is not easy for any nation. It is especially difficult for a democracy with a constitution shaped in earlier—and different—times. That of the United States having been arrived at by discussion, often acrimonious, and with eventual compromises among differing representatives, was disputable from the start. It was ratified in some state conventions by slight majorities—meaning that nearly half the delegates to these meetings did not approve at least some of its provisions.

Disagreements continued, but new proposals always threatened the compromises reached at Philadelphia and precipitated renewed quarrels about the same issues. Because such dissensions were dreaded, and because new concessions might disturb old positions, actual amendments were seldom possible. Besides, the provisions accumulated interested supporters who learned how to bend them to their advantage or to prevent any disadvantageous changes. Among these supporters were most members of the legal profession. A protective attitude toward what existed soon developed and strengthened as the Constitution grew older. Practitioners and judges surrounded the document with an aura of near-sacredness—the terms of that sacredness being their own elucidations of meaning. It was a more potent interest too because all the judiciary and a large proportion of every legislature belonged to the legal guild.

Still, conditions do change, and what has happened must eventually be recognized and some accommodation made. There was often a choice between amending the Constitution and allowing it to be warped into a different shape by general agreement to ignore departures from its clauses as written. New practices grew up without any attempt to reconcile them with the document or the system it established.

There was, however, a more favored alternative. The Court found in the Constitution the necessary elasticity to permit departures. When this method was adopted, or allowed to develop, the makers of these interpretations naturally became all-important. Only an inexperienced observer would have expected justices to understand the importance of systemic integrity. Besides, their selection was made in a politicized atmosphere that became worse as the Constitution became more obsolete. The interpreters departed more and more widely from literal meanings. The best that could be done—or that a democracy could hope to have done if amendment was not possible—was to have constitutional implications entrusted to a highly qualified and nonpartisan body with respect for the national interest and fairness in adversary situations.

The Supreme Court has demonstrated how unrealistic it was to look for this holism among judges or for attitudes free of recognizable bias. Prejudices were always quite apparent, and, as a result, the Court was often a center of controversy. Nevertheless, with the support of the profession it maintained its prestige and continued to shape the law to its view of social and economic conditions. The process was slow and uneven;

also it had marked periods of conservative and liberal bias; but it remained the sole source of generally accepted constitutional change. Professionals even made a virtue of the process. They spoke of a "living constitution," meaning one that was freely changed. What made it live, of course, was the invention of new meanings by the justices. The Framers themselves must be held responsible for constricting the methods of accommodation and indirectly for the establishment of the Court as the agency for legitimizing new activities and novel situations. The word "interpretation" appears nowhere in the Constitution, but once the Court had invented it there was no going back. It was inevitable that some time a chief justice would inform the descendants of the people who made the Constitution that it is what the justices say it is.

To find and seat justices with the requisite qualifications for such a responsibility it would have been necessary to provide for appointment in such a way as to ensure that only nonpartisan and distinguished legalists would be eligible and that they would owe their appointments to a source free of any intent to influence their subsequent judgments, but qualifications were not specified in the Constitution, and appointments were entrusted to what turned out to be the most partisan of all sources—the president. The only assurance of impartiality was the protection judges were given after taking office. It had been provided that they should hold their appointments "during good behavior" and that their compensations should not be reduced while they continued to serve. This, however, protected both the wise and the foolish.

Whatever the Framers were thinking of when this clause was adopted, it was clearly not expected that the justices would be rewriters of the Constitution. For this purpose the two separate processes spoken of were provided, something that would not have been done unless amendments had been contemplated. It cannot have been foreseen, if this was the expectation, that one of these would be extremely difficult and the other practically impossible. Yet this did prove to be true. The one method yielded only some twenty-six amendments in nearly two centuries, ten of them the Bill of Rights promised in the ratification conventions. The other method resulted in none at all. When the provision that was to have this consequence was written Gouverneur Morris must have been dozing.

Article V, the amending clause, reads as follows:

> The Congress, whenever two thirds of both Houses shall deem it necessary, shall propose Amendments to this Constitution, or, on the Application of the Legislatures of two thirds of the several States, shall call a Convention for proposing Amendments, which, in either Case, shall be valid to all Intents and Purposes, as Part of this Constitution, when ratified by the Legislatures of three fourths of the several States, or by Conventions in three fourths thereof, as the one or the other Mode of Ratification may be proposed by the Congress; Provided that no Amendment which may be made prior to the Year One thousand eight hundred and eight shall in any Manner affect the first and fourth Clauses in the Ninth Section of the first Article; and that no State, without its Consent, shall be deprived of its equal Suffrage in the Senate.

Only two amendments in the Constitution's history can be said to have affected the structure of government. One changed the method of electing senators and the other limited presidents to no more than two terms in office. The others had to do with citizens' rights or electoral procedures, mostly, although two had to do with the manufacture, sale and transportation of intoxicating liquors, these being first prohibited then a few years later freed from the prohibition. None really touched the powers of any branch or affected the principles of opposed checks or concurrent sovereignty.

This must be said to have been a small yield of accommodation to circumstances in so changeable a time. Constitutional government being of a particular kind, an obsolete charter would obviously defeat the purpose in having one at all. That it did not become quite hopelessly irrelevant was owed to that freedom of interpretation just spoken of, not contemplated in the original agreement. It has become the main reliance for adaptation to continuing change, apart, of course, from the carrying on of activities not mentioned and so not prohibited. These are immense in number but safe only so long as they do not come under scrutiny.

When the Framers devised their system they provided that the Court should possess "the judicial power of the United States." They added only that this power should extend "to all cases in law and equity arising under the constitution, the laws of the United States, and treaties made under their authority...." It was not said, or even hinted, that the Constitution might be altered as cases were decided; and since the word "interpretation" did not appear, it was obviously expected that alterations would be made only by amendment. That this was the expectation is supported by the extensive subordinating of the Court to controls by the Congress. The number of its members could be specified, and even its jurisdiction was to be determined by "such regulations as the congress shall make." The justices seemed confined to deciding whether opinions of inferior courts brought to it on appeal were within their jurisdiction and consistent with the justice mentioned in the preamble.

Hamilton, commenting on the Court, said that it would be weak in the inevitable interbranch conflicts to come and for that reason needed secure appointments and salaries. He suggested that these defenses might have been stronger. Even before ratification he foresaw that as cases arose there would be interpretations. He said this in *The Federalist* (No. 78) without elaborating the argument. A few years later he did explain, when asked by Washington for his opinion on the bill establishing the Bank of the United States. Interpretation was not a specified power, he said, it did not need to be; it was necessary to the general welfare and welfare was a stated purpose in the preamble; any measure to secure it was therefore necessarily implied.

Jefferson, also asked for his opinion on this same bill, gave advice the precise opposite of Hamilton's, thereby becoming the first and most rigid of the theoretical strict constructionists. Hamilton's belief in flexibility would be the line followed by nationalists throughout the coming years. Even Jefferson, however, when he became president, would discover that the Constitution was confining. Here it should be recalled that a remarkably permissive clause had been added to the legislative powers, apparently at the last moment. It used the expansive expression "necessary and proper."

> The Congress shall have the power . . . to make all laws which shall be necessary and proper for carrying into execution the foregoing powers, and all other powers vested by this constitution in the

government of the United States or in any department or officer thereof.

For the Congress the Framers laid down the eighteen specifications in Section 8 of Article II, the last being the permission, just cited, to make further laws to effectuate the preceding seventeen directives. Also, there were further specifications, applying mostly to the Congress, in Section 9. Altogether it was a list of formidable scope and considerable detail. The powers of the legislature were meant to be dominant and comprehensive.

For the president there were fewer prescriptions. In addition to making appointments and negotiating treaties, he was "to take care that the laws are faithfully executed." He was, besides, to be commander-in-chief of the armed forces and might veto legislation (although his veto could be overridden by a two-thirds vote). Also he might make certain nominations for office, but these were subject to confirmation by the Senate. And because he was to make treaties (provided two-thirds of the senators concurred), and nominate "ambassadors, other public ministers, and consuls," he was to have an important but not exclusive role in the conduct of foreign relations. There was the caveat that in these matters he should have the "advice and consent" of the Senate.

As for the judicial branch, there were even more meagre directives than for the presidency and much more restricted ones than those detailed for the legislature. Why did the Framers have so much better defined intentions for the legislative than for the executive branch, and why almost none at all for the Court? It may again have been because resistance to British rule had centered in the state legislatures before the rebellion and because the courts had generally been dominated by the British governors. At any rate, the subordination of the other branches to the legislature seems not to have been seriously opposed.

These curious contrasts were made worse by the adoption, soon after ratification, of the first series of amendments, the Bill of Rights. These were further directives intended to protect the liberties of citizens from the encroachments of government. They were adopted as a result of objections made and promises offered when ratification seemed likely to be withheld in several states. The first began "the Congress shall make no law . . ." and all were prohibitions. Their scope and their brevity made certain that disputes about their meanings would be even more likely than for the provisions concerning the executive, but none would ever be clarified by amendment.

The Court, in fact, had no discernible marching orders, merely something called "jurisdiction." This was original only in cases affecting "ambassadors, other public ministers, and consuls" and those involving a state; in all others it was appellate. The members of the first Court hardly knew where to start or what to do if they did start, and for ten years they were asked to do very little, so little that while in office the first chief justice, John Jay, was twice a candidate for the governorship of New York and spent a year in England on a diplomatic mission. Samuel Chase made it impossible for the Court to meet during one whole term because he was engaged in partisan electioneering. He was impeached by the Jeffersonian House, but escaped conviction. Altogether the Court only became important when John Marshall became its chief justice.

Meanwhile the Congress had passed several judiciary acts intended to fill out the lacking instructions. The justification for this legislation was the clause concerning the establishment of lower courts. There were, it was said, to be such of these "as the congress may from time to time ordain and establish."

There is another puzzling difficulty about this passage, one that applies also to others. It was said in several instances that "the congress may, by law" do a number of things, but "laws" are not completed until approved by the president. Was this exclusion of the president simply an oversight, or was there to be a category of legislation not requiring presidential consent? There is no more satisfactory and conclusive way of resolving this uncertainty than of resolving others. The Congress does pass "resolutions" not requiring presidential consent, and the initiation of an amendment is an exclusively congressional act, but concurrent resolutions have always been recognized as expressions of opinion rather than legislation. There is no light on the Framers' intention.

Concerning the scope of the judicial power, complications arose because of differences between nationalists and localists. It should be noted that the Framers did not anticipate the formation of political parties and made no provision for them, although all during the Convention's debates, a division was apparent. It is a source of confusion that those who thought of themselves as nationalists or unionists soon were calling themselves Federalists and those who stood for states' rights and later for "strict construction" adopted the name Democratic-Republican. Only later did the "Republican" disappear and only the "Democratic" remain. Confusion was compounded when, in mid-nineteenth century, the former nationalists would drop an interregnum name "Whig" and begin to call themselves Republicans. This, however, would be when Jeffersonians were no longer presidents. When Hamilton, Madison, and Jay wrote their defense of the Constitution and called it *The Federalist,* it was a misnomer; none of them believed in federalism, and their papers were unionist documents—that is to say, their contention was that the Union would be consolidated by ratification of the Constitution. Did they adopt the federalist name with intent to deceive? At any rate they created confusion.

The Federalists, having a majority in the first sessions of the new Congress, adopted a statute providing for national courts at two levels. There were to be district courts in every state and three circuit courts. This act of 1789 would be revised both before and after Jefferson succeeded to the presidency in 1801, the revisions being determined by changing majority views of the Court's position in the governmental system.

The Congress may have exceeded its warrant in passing these comprehensive laws establishing and revising the judiciary. The acts went beyond the Constitution's clause empowering the legislature "to constitute courts inferior to the Supreme Court." It was a chief justice, however, not the Congress, who grossly enlarged the constitutional directive. In 1801, John Marshall had been appointed by the defeated president, John Adams, only one month before giving way to Jefferson. The appointment was an affront to the incoming president, since Marshall was a determined Federalist and the Federalists had lost the election. Nevertheless, since judges held office for life unless impeached, he would retain his position through several presidencies and consistently oppose the Jeffersonian ambition to diminish federal power and enlarge that of the states.

Following the construction suggested by Hamilton, Marshall asserted that the Court could say what the Constitution meant. What the Congress had done was to say how the judiciary was to be organized. Except by implication neither the Court nor the Congress had any justification for these actions, but, as we shall see, Marshall's move was the bolder.

The justices, according to the Marshall doctrine, stated fact when they "interpreted." Whatever anyone else might think, even members of the other branches, the Court was to have the last word. This wholly ignored the taking of oaths by those others "to support the constitution"—presumably as they understood it—but from then on the justices stood on the Marshall dictum and were able to sustain the position.

The implied powers were thus resorted to in these extraordinary seizures by the Congress and the Court. Amendment was not necessary if each branch, as it felt the necessity, could reach for and use the powers it wanted, with no more real support than its own assumption that they were needed and were derived from some constitutional clause. However strained the imputation, reinforced by the sweeping final clause of Section 8, Article I, containing the words "necessary and proper," they prevailed. That is, they prevailed unless on occasion they were met by a contending derivation. That might come from the Congress, or it might come from the president. Occasionally the resulting conflict was embarrassingly public. More often it was intense and unremitting but too technical for general understanding.

Early instances of extension by implication will be briefly described in due course; but it may be said here that the effect was to begin the process of alteration, justified by citing the need for a "living" constitution. Legitimate authentication was thus given up and the proud claim of the preamble's first words abandoned. It could no longer honestly be said that the Constitution owed its existence to "the people."

5: Amendment

The uniqueness of the document adopted by the Philadelphia convention is often remarked. The authors of
The Federalist did claim pridefully that the Constitution
was the only national charter in existence drawn up by
representatives of a people and approved by them in
referenda; all others, they said, had been imposed from
above. Those for whom a system of government and a
higher law were being provided had neither participated
nor given consent.*

This was true then but is no longer. Several—not
many—nations have adopted constitutions in some variety of such a process. It is true that referenda accepting
them have often been of doubtful validity, and so they
have had only the superficial appearance of legitimacy.
Most are still of this kind, drawn up overnight at the
instance of whoever has happened to be in power, and
changed without ceremony by decree if any of their
clauses proved inconvenient. As Americans would view
them these are not constitutions at all. Theirs, ratified in
specially elected conventions, is still unusual because of
its authentication; but another difference has come to
characterize it; and this is not so praiseworthy. What is
most notable after two centuries, is its proven resistance

The Federalist, No. 38.

to substantive revision by legitimate means. Other nations with similar charters have had a succession of them, a new one following every civic convulsion; and, when not wholly supplanted, they have frequently been revised. That of the United States having remained essentially unchanged for almost two hundred years, can indeed be praised for longevity; but that virtue is eroded by an increasing disregard for its injunctions.

Even the Civil War, more than seventy years after its adoption, did not result in structural changes to define the meaning of concurrent sovereignty. That is what the war was about; but it resulted only in an enlarged definition of certain citizens' rights, especially those who had before been slaves. The Southern states' assertion of the right to secede was rejected; but the Constitution was not amended to forbid it. Except for civil rights, the states nominally still had all the powers they had asserted before their defeat as a confederacy.

The fact is that, like those of other nations, the constitution of the United States has been altered. It has been done, however, by other methods than amendment. Although textually the document has been left essentially intact, its clauses—or many of them—are no longer taken to mean what the Framers intended. Constructions have had much the same effect as amendment might have had. The difficulty is that these have not been approved by the people, only by a majority of nine justices. Consequently they are never quite legitimate or quite permanent.

Clearly the Framers had not intended that the Constitution should be impervious to amendment. As has been noted, they provided two processes for this. If both proved difficult afterwards, this was not intended either, although it was indeed considered that revisions should not be so easy as to be amenable to sudden popular caprice. About this, concern was repeatedly expressed during the deliberations. They intended that the higher law should be resistant to changes forced by such demagogues as Daniel Shays.

As the delegates approached the finish of their work the worst of the divisive differences were resolved in uneasy compromises, so uneasy, in fact, that delegates like Mason and Randolph of Virginia, two of the most active participants, refused to sign. This remaining residue of dissent was so prevalent, even among those who did sign, that the omission of a better device for amendment seems strange indeed.

Objections and alternate proposals had been given up only in the interest of achieving the union believed essential to the continuance of the still insecure nation. There were those who had wanted more central power; others who had wanted less. Some had feared the new executive and some had thought the presidency much too weak. Some, representing the small states, had confronted the large ones with demands for renewed recognition of their traditional independence. The nationalists considered that this would make union impossible.

The compromises must have been regarded as temporary. Such strong advocates as are revealed in Madison's notes cannot have abandoned their positions altogether. The claim of the small states for guarantees of equality, more troublesome than other differences, had resulted in a second legislative house, where all states, large and small, would have equal representation. It was accepted by the majority only reluctantly in order to prevent the smaller states from calling their delegates home. It was while this controversy was at its worst that Washington wrote to Hamilton, who was in New York, that he feared imminent failure because delegates with "local views" would not give way. He was too pessimistic. The suggestion was accepted and the meeting passed to other issues.

Discussions at the Pennsylvania state house were sometimes heated, and they ended more often in compromise than in conversion. If the holders of determined views still hoped to prevail in time, they must have foreseen amendments. Yet there was no such serious consideration of the process as there was about many other issues. On July 11, early in the meeting, a resolution providing for amendment without participation by the Congress was considered. Several members objected to this proposed exclusion, but a worried Mason urged it and was supported by Randolph. Mason's argument was recorded by Madison:

> The plan now to be formed will certainly be defective as the Confederation has been found on trial to be. Amendments therefore will be necessary, and it will be better to provide for them in an easy, regular, and constitutional way than to trust to chance and violence. It would be improper to require the consent of the national legislature, because they may abuse their power, and refuse their consent on that very account. The opportunity for such an abuse may be the fault of the Constitution calling for amendment.

It is not entirely clear what Mason meant. It is evident that some discussion must have preceded his statement. He probably preferred that amendments should originate with and be ratified by the *state* legislatures, excluding the *national* legislature, but he may have been voicing the same view as Tom Paine who, in *The Rights of Man*, said that "to suppose any government can be a party in a compact with the whole people is to suppose it to have existence before it can have the right to exist."

Madison noted that at this point there was "postponement," something usual in the Convention when agreement was not readily reached. However, only the participation of the national legislature was left for future decision; the rest of the clause was accepted "nem. con." There was no dissent from the future need for amendment, but there was also no commitment to participation by others than legislators.

There is a further entry in Madison's notes on September 10, when the Convention was nearing its end. On that day Gerry moved to reconsider the article providing that legislatures in two-thirds of the states might require the Congress to call an amending convention. He asked whether this was a proper arrangement since a majority in a convention called by the Congress could bind the states to "innovations that might subvert the state constitutions altogether." This again expressed an antinationalist position. The localists were still wary.

Hamilton seconded Gerry's proposal for reconsideration but with something quite different in mind. The state legislatures, he said, "would not apply for alterations but with a view to increase their own powers." The national legislature would be the first to perceive and would be the most sensible to the necessity for change. Since the people would decide anyway it would be best to leave initiation to their representatives in the Congress. If this was a suggestion that referenda might be held it was not pursued and it would hardly be consistent with Hamilton's well-known elitist views.

On September 15 a rewritten clause was discussed. Sherman still feared, as Gerry did, that three-fourths of the states might be brought to do things fatal to some of the others, and Mason insisted that the plan was "exceptionable and dangerous." This was another expression of his fear that national power was being enlarged; if amendment were to depend on the Congress, none of the proper kind would ever be obtained by the people. "If the government should become oppressive, as he verily believed would be the case," there would be no changes.

Sherman joined the debate, also speaking for the small states as he had on other issues. They must, he said, have further protection, and he suggested a proviso that "no state, without its consent be affected in its internal police, or be deprived of its equal suffrage in the Senate." Madison objected that if a beginning was made "of admitting such special provisos every state would insist on them, for their boundaries, their exports, etc." Nevertheless Sherman and his allies prevailed in this instance, and Article V, as finally adopted, had the curious last sentence providing that "no state, without its consent, shall be deprived of its equal suffrage in the Senate." It occured to no one, apparently, that this established a contradiction, or if it did occur, there was no recognition that, like other provisions, protection for the Senate would be subject to revision unless the intention was to set limits to amendment. This was a denial of the people's originating powers. The uneasiness of politicians from the smaller states may have been somewhat allayed, but the contradiction of prohibiting a particular amendment in a clause providing generally for amendment was obvious. The concession was purely political.

The arrangement assigning the initiative to the legislative branches of the states and the nation was thus adopted with the consent of all but a few who wanted initiatives to be located elsewhere, presumably in a people's petition of some sort. That Hamilton should have said, as he did, that the people would decide anyway, and that he should have argued for origination in the Congress seems especially strange. He might have been expected, considering his usual views, to contend that the Court would be best fitted to originate amendments; after all, its members would be the first to discover defects, ambiguities, or omissions. Evidently, however, he, and the other Federalists, felt compelled to accept origination in the *national* legislature as the alternative to the *state* legislatures. He might well have considered that the president would find his powers deficient and ought to have a part in the amending process. By then, however, the choice had been narrowed and nothing more was done except to admit both national and state legislatures to the procedure.

Some further enlightenment is furnished by passages written by Hamilton in *The Federalist,* during the months following the Convention's close. The argument in those papers was intended to persuade the ratifying convention in New York (and hopefully the one still to come in Virginia) that the charter was a practical one, calculated to protect the interests of those important citizens who would do the ratifying. Beyond this, however, the grand object was to secure the Union. For this purpose all the positions taken by the Convention's majority were defended. Many of these Hamilton had consistently opposed all his life and truckling to the states' righters must have been especially galling. In this interest he supported the amendment clause, although he cannot have thought the matter ought to be left entirely to legislative branches. But he probably had less difficulty with it because other issues then being discussed seemed more important. That its priority was low is shown by its treatment. He spoke of it first in Number 43 of *The Federalist,* under the head of "miscellaneous powers," after he had written copiously in defense of other provisions. It was, in fact, eighth in a list of nine.

What he said was this:

> That useful alterations will be suggested by experience, could not but be foreseen. It was requisite, therefore, that a mode for introducing them should be provided. The mode preferred by the convention seems to be stamped with every mark of propriety. It guards equally against that extreme facility which would render the constitution too mutable; and that extreme difficulty which might perpetuate its discovered faults. It moreover equally enables the general and the state governments to originate the amendment of errors as they may be pointed out by the experience on one side or on the other.

He went on to speak of that inherently contradictory tag attached to the clause:

> The exception in favour of the equality of suffrage in the senate was probably meant as a palladium to the residuary sovereignty of the states, implied and secured by that principle of representation in one branch of the legislature, and was probably insisted on by the states particularly attached to that equality. . . .

Amendment was again referred to in the very last of the papers, published just as the New York delegates were about to convene at Poughkeepsie for the ratifying convention. Hamilton's argument then, however, was prompted by a new threat. After some eight months of controversy about ratification, the antifederalists had retreated to the position that since the Philadelphia draft was admittedly imperfect, its adoption ought to be put off until it could be improved. This, Hamilton objected, would leave the country in a deepening crisis, already near fatal. He then pointed out that amendments made *after* ratification would require the consent of only nine states whereas those made *before* ratification would require the unanimous consent of all thirteen, something almost impossible to achieve, and not likely anyway to improve on the results reached in Philadelphia.

Jay, who because of a long illness, had made only a few contributions to *The Federalist,* now reinforced this position in a separately published pamphlet, "An Address to the People of New York." He added nothing new, however, merely affirming that amendments had been adequately provided for in the proposed Constitution. Hamilton and Jay, together, apparently persuaded their contemporaries. New York, in the Poughkeepsie convention, did ratify the Constitution. There was abrasive opposition from Governor Clinton and his followers; nevertheless the consenting majority was sufficient. Several suggestions for future changes were made, but it was not insisted that these should be made before ratification or that they should in any way be made easier.

It was left that way when the new government began its operations in 1789.

6: Inter-Branch Bargains

Amendments of substantial importance having been made nearly impossible, there did have to be some way of accommodating the supreme law to a developing society. One way was to ignore innovations until they were challenged; and another was to recognize the Supreme Court's authority to expand the Constitution's over-brief clauses or to fill its numerous lacunae.

Both ways became customary. It was simply assumed that anything not mentioned in the Constitution was not prohibited—either to governments or to private citizens. Of course this offended such strict constructionists as Jefferson and, later on, the active secessionists, who wanted to escape federal authority altogether, but a nation expanding in every direction could not manage itself within the Framers' structure. And until a case made its way through legal difficulties to the Supreme Court there would be no decision; as a result, multitudes of activities unmentioned in the Constitution went on unimpeded. Even in Washington's time an issue of this sort arose over the establishment of Hamilton's controversial national bank but many others would develop as the country grew, especially during and after the Civil War. Even when many of these had to be controlled for sheer defense against increasing abuses of economic power there was no amendment to allow regulation by delegation.

The second means of expansion—by way of Court opinion—was the more important because of its imputed legitimacy. Once successfully begun, the Court could find innumerable ways to use such phrases as "necessary and proper," "regulation of commerce among the several states," "affected with the public interest" and "with all deliberate speed." There was some difficulty about applying these to other activities than those mentioned as congressional or presidential powers, but the permissions eventually extended to surprisingly unlike enterprises.

In 1794 the Court was rebuked by the eleventh amendment restricting its power to entertain any suit against one of the states, but thereafter it attained such a position of authority that its inferences were not again seriously questioned. For instance, what businesses were engaged in interstate commerce became so tenuous an identification that practically no activity except the smallest businesses remained intrastate. They either were or were not affected with a public interest as the Court determined. No amendment provided directives, and the justices resorted to case by case opinions reflecting their particular views. Statements of principle could seldom be agreed on. Future litigants were often no more certain about their causes than before decisions had been made. The Court, by avoiding wide pronouncements, and keeping its interpretations narrow, ran less risk of general challenges to its authority. Only seldom would questions about allocated powers come to the Court for settlement. It would creep rather than hasten toward its final assertion of supremacy among the branches.

One unfortunate confusion was at once exposed when the government began operations. "Executive departments" were mentioned in the Constitution, as were "officers of the United States." Concerning these it was said that the president could require the opinion of their heads "upon any subject relating to the duties of their respective offices." It was also said that he might appoint such of them as were "not otherwise provided for" and which "shall be established by law." What did this mean? Officers could hardly be appointed without first having had their positions created. Nothing whatever was said about the procedure for this. To make matters worse, the same passage went on to say that the Congress might "by law vest the appointment of such inferior officers, as they think proper, in the president alone, in the courts of law, or in the heads of departments."

It may be recalled that certain departments already existed. Under the governance of the Continental Congress, there had been organized agencies devoted to foreign affairs, war, and finance. There was also a legal adviser. Washington had no immediate desire for others. Some years before he had become president, single heads had been substituted for the commissions previously in charge of these, but if he was to be the chief executive it was necessary for him to know whether they were to continue their responsibility to the Congress or were to be his subordinates. He could not be at all certain what was meant by the Constitution's baffling clauses.

He might well have demanded clarification. In a simple hortatory passage he was enjoined to "take care that the laws be faithfully executed." How could he do that if the Congress could vest the appointment of his subordinates in "the courts of law" or in "the heads of departments?" How, indeed, could he execute the laws if the only clause defining his relation to department heads allowed him only to require their opinions in writing? This would seem to visualize such a remote supervision that "faithful execution" would be impossible. His embarrassment will be discussed later.

This early avoidance of amendment as a way to clarify the lapses and mistakes made by Gouverneur Morris and his committee on style ought to have been seen, by Madison at least, who was a member of the first Congress, as a serious matter, but if it was he did not say so. That was the time when the Constitution was having its earliest trials. Simple omissions and contradictions ought to have been corrected at once. It would have required no more than a few words, but from that time on the branches felt free to agree among themselves on all the allocations of power not well defined in the Constitution. In the long history to come there would never be an amendment clarifying such an issue. If the Constitution did not forbid the doing of something, each branch could, whenever it chose, push out into the many opening opportunities. When opposed they simply bargained for position. This was the situation as well of private persons and organizations. In a society rapidly becoming more complicated than that of 1787, each of them, studying the Constitution and finding no guidance, simply proceeded in its own interest.

The repeated aggressions of each branch, when resented and opposed by another, is sometimes defended as a way of arriving at a practical balance, just as the same procedures are defended by classical economists for businesses. Each, it is said, will in this way discover what are the limits of its powers—what it can or cannot do. This view has only superficial validity in either area, but especially in government. For one thing, there are dangers in interbranch bargaining so serious that several times they have come close to destroying the tripartite structure. How completely dependent that structure is on precarious self-restraint has repeatedly been demonstrated by the aggressive behavior of contending officials, and the danger has not grown less with progress into more complicated governmental responsibilities.

Wars have been particularly dangerous times. At their beginning there has always been an immediate grant of extraordinary powers to the president. Or if they have not been granted he has assumed them anyway. Jefferson did this when Barbary pirates became a nuisance; Lincoln did it when civil war was imminent; so did Roosevelt when he established sea patrols in anticipation of hostilities; Truman had doubtful approval for his Korean venture; and Vietnam offered a text-book of illustrations. When, however, wars have required sacrifices the Congress has balked and limited, or attempted to limit, the assumed powers. It happened with Lincoln and his successor Andrew Johnson; it happened with Roosevelt; and it happened with Truman, Johnson, and Nixon. Timely compromise has prevented conclusive victory for any branch. There could be none for any but the legislature, but its resorts to the finality of impeachment have been infrequent. Its numbers have made the necessary majorities difficult to assemble where presidents were concerned. Still, the possibility has given the overweening ones something to consider.

The Framers, who contrived checks and balances, ought to have imposed clearer limits for each. They might well have prevented congressional invasion of the executive and, as well, made sure that the president would not proceed, even in emergency, to try beyond tolerance congressional compliance. Even more important, the Court might have been enjoined from becoming the definer of powers for all branches including itself.

Real damage has been narrowly escaped on several occasions and each escape has offered lessons concerning the Constitution, but none of them has resulted in amendment. The general effect has been to heighten the danger from each crisis.

If it is hard to excuse the Framers for leaving the Constitution in such ambiguous condition, it is also hard to excuse Washington for failing to demand that his powers be better defined, not by a fragile bargain but by amendment that would make them secure, even when legislators or judges for some reason became actively hostile.

It is doubly unfortunate that although the Constitution was generally recognized as experimental, and although changes must have been expected, its more confusing clauses were not clarified—unfortunate because although the arrangements of 1789 allowed Washington to go on reasonably well, they established at the same time the belief that the way to proceed when it was impossible to determine what the Constitution required was to settle the immediate question, however important, by negotiation rather than by amendment. That is, of course, why amendments became infrequent after the first twelve were ratified. None were needed so long as constitutional meanings could be compromised when inconsistent with one another.

There would be weak presidents who would give way to pressure, even while recognizing that they had a national constituency. There would be frightened Congresses whose members would simply abdicate in crisis, allowing presidents to assume emergency powers likely to be surrendered only reluctantly when the crisis had passed—or perhaps never wholly given up.

These actions were made easier because congressmen discovered almost at once the possibility and convenience of anonymity. Members' votes were not recorded. So if things went well they could take credit for not interfering. If things went badly they could excoriate the president. What was convenient for individuals, however, was bad for the Congress as a whole. It would steadily lose power to both president and Court, only occasionally working itself into rages when presidents lost popular favor. These were the dangerous times for the structure of government. The Congress had been given the tool of impeachment and sometime might use it to punish a political enemy rather than to protect the principle of separate but interdependent powers. Among the checks and balances only impeachment was absolute; all the others were conditioned. And its use was consigned to a branch so situated as to be the natural enemy of executives.

As for the Court, it seems to have had a relative immunity to rebuke. This would be hard to account for if its approach to "supremacy" had not been so circumspect, and, perhaps, if a majority of the legislature had not always belonged to the legal profession and had the traditional exaggerated respect for the elite of that guild.

7: Alternatives

Although the amending clause was defended in *The Federalist*, this can have been no more than part of the authors' general support for ratification when the outcome was doubtful. Hamilton, Madison, and Jay were not very well hidden as Publius; the elite of New York were too few and too intimately associated for the customary pamphleteering signatures to be effective. The prestige of two New York lawyers belonging to the city's prominent families must have had a decisive effect on opinion. Madison, also, the third author, in New York as a member of the expiring Congress, belonged to the similar elite of Virginia. Knowledge of their general purpose makes it impossible to say, really, whether the three authors, arguing ardently the virtues of the proposed Constitution, did really think the amending clause adequate.

They admitted quite frankly, in other passages, that imperfect men could not be expected to produce perfect instruments, and that changes would certainly be found necessary in future. They did not indicate what they thought those changes might be, but their attitudes in the controversies of the years just past were well enough known and they would naturally hope that the positions they had not been able to persuade the delegates at Philadelphia to adopt would in time make their

way into the Constitution. If, however, they did have
hopes of this sort, it is curious that they acceded—apparently without argument—to a method of amending
so unlikely to result in the substantial changes they
must have thought necessary.

How, then, account for their carelessness about this
matter at the Convention? The answer must be that
they were more interested in union than in anything
else. A large part of *The Federalist* was devoted to
warnings about the consequences of separateness and
the contention that ratification was essential to the
future integrity of the nation. They dissembled. They
evaded embarrassing issues. They twisted the meanings
of such clauses as were arousing fears. They exaggerated
the future independence of the states within the proposed federation. They minimized the powers assigned
to the central government. Clearly they considered the
sacrifice of accuracy justified if it contributed to the
establishment of union.

This, however, does not explain why at the Convention they consented without objection to an amending
clause they must have disapproved. A clue to that is to
be found elsewhere, specifically in Number 78 of *The
Federalist* where Hamilton examined the judiciary. In
that essay he took some pains to explain certain privileges granted the Court's judges. He noted that the
judicial would be the weakest of the branches, unable to
hold its own in contests sure to arise with the others.
Both the president and the Congress had been awarded
powers to shape and control the Court—the president
was to make appointments (subject to senatorial confirmation) and the Congress was to designate inferior
courts and determine jurisdiction. Between them they
would fix its budget. These serious disabilities were

compensated for, Hamilton said, by providing that the judges should be appointed "during good behavior" and should have compensations that could not be diminished during their continuation in office. These provisions, he argued, would make it difficult for the Congress or the president to influence decisions.

If his defense of this arrangement is put together with another passage on the same essay, it begins to appear why he may not have been much concerned about formal amendment:

> The complete independence of the courts of justice is peculiarly essential in a limited constitution. By a limited constitution I understand one which contains certain specified exceptions to the legislative authority.... Limitations of this kind can be preserved in practice no other way than through the medium of the courts of justice; *whose duty it must be to declare all the acts contrary to the manifest tenor of the constitution void ...* [emphasis added].

Hamilton evidently realized that this was a startling claim, as of course it was, and immediately went on to argue—unconvincingly—that this did not actually imply judicial supremacy. There was danger, he pointed out, that the legislature might be the determiner of its own powers and that the construction it put upon them "might be conclusive upon other departments." It could not have been intended, he went on, that the representatives of the people should substitute their will for that of the people themselves. Only the judiciary could keep the legislature within its assigned limits:

> The interpretation of the laws is the proper and peculiar province of the courts. A constitution is,

in fact, and must be regarded by the judges, as a fundamental law. It therefore belongs to them to ascertain its meaning as well as the meaning of any particular act proceeding from the legislative body.

There followed the final ingenious passage making *judicial supremacy* seem only *constitutional supremacy* and therefore unassailable:

Nor does this conclusion by any means suppose a superiority of the judicial to the legislative power. It only supposes that the power of the people is superior to both; and that where the will of the legislature, declared in its statutes, stands in opposition to that of the people, declared in its constitution, the judges ought to be governed by the latter, rather than the former. They ought to regulate their decisions by the fundamental laws, rather than by those which are not fundamental.

Hamilton notwithstanding, if judicial interpretations have not kept the Constitution from obsolescence, then the processes of amendment ought to have been more carefully considered. That the amending clause has indeed proved insufficient is suggested by the fact, already noted, that no alterations of substantial importance, such as would have accommodated the Constitution to changing circumstances, have ever been made. Insufficiency is also suggested by the bare figures of resort to the process. If the first ten amendments are excluded as having been adopted in circumstances that make them almost part of the original document, such actions have come at an average of less than one in a decade. There were several just after the Civil War when the southern states were not yet readmitted to the Union (13, 14, and 15) all having to do with the issues of the war; but the first of these was not ratified until sixty-one years after the previous one. That is a long gap, and after 1870 there were no more until 1913—another gap of forty-three years. After 1933 there were only two in the next twenty-eight years.

Argument proceeding from mere periodicity does not prove that the process is too difficult, but it cannot be denied that this was a time of vast and often violent social and economic changes, and that it was also a time when the Constitution was construed in such ways as to alter seriously many of its clauses. The question would have to be asked: Had a satisfactory way been found to revise the higher law without actually amending it?

The Constitution, after its long existence, still commanded enormous respect of a kind hard to define. It was regarded as the heart and soul of the American political order. Officials, on taking office, not only swore to uphold it but uniformly referred to it respectfully and professed to be its ardent defenders. It said something that this was done by those whose policies, if implemented, would have been diametrically opposed. This veneration, however, had not been confined to those who merely sought the cover of patriotism; it had also characterized the opinions of the judiciary. The judges, of course, had good reason to rest on the sacredness of the document since they could make of it, within credible limits, whatever they wanted. True, they had found in it the justification for such different positions that the claim to be expounding the same document at different times could hardly be credited. That nevertheless they *were* credited suggests a kind of silent conspiracy to agree that something was so that obviously was not so. There were defenders of this procedure. They were the ones who called the body of precedent being created by the Court the "living Constitution."

One interesting explanation sometimes made for the secure position of the Court is that the universally recognized symbol of the American ethos is consigned to it as guardian and exponent. The Constitution occupies a place much like the royal family in Britain. Presidents ought to be such a symbol, and a few have had something of this charisma, but too often they have lacked the qualities necessary to sustain this regard. They have become politicized; often little more than half the electorate has voted for them; and many have been mercilessly attacked while in office. The Constitution is never disparaged. There is frequent dispute about the meaning of its provisions and Court decisions frequently modify these meanings; but it remains the one continuing universally respected national symbol. The Court shelters in its prestige.

This is perhaps a sufficient explanation of the relationship between Court and Constitution, but skeptics call attention to several reasons why it ought not to be so. One is historical. There have been periods, well-defined ones, when the Court has been consistently on one or the other side of a rather uncertain demarcation between conservatism and liberalism. This seldom corresponded in later years with the earlier controversy between strict and loose constructionists, a quarrel that belonged back before the Civil War. Then Jefferson and his Democratic Republicans were on one side and Hamilton and the Federalists—with their successors—on the other. It had to do with political issues. What more typically divided constitutionalists after the era of business regulation began, was conservatism and liberalism in economic matters. The Court was conservative until the 1930's when Roosevelt appointees became a majority. What the Constitution permitted the government to do in regulating business and in advancing social welfare was seen in opposite ways by the Court during these periods. The Nixon appointees changed it again.

This in itself would controvert any claim to the infallibility attributed to it by supporters. But the skeptics— who seemed to be fewer and fewer as time passed—had other reservations. They could point to the large number of decisions reached by close votes among the justices. Evidently some of them did not share the infallibility of others; when matters of national importance depended upon the decision of one justice, in a five to four vote, infallibility seemed, to say the least, questionable. There were other reasons for doubt. One was that the "living Constitution" was being created by justices who, being appointed, represented no one and nothing; and certainly not the people who were the legitimate constitution-makers. Further, that their conclusions were not subjected to referendum or even to specially selected ratifying conventions as had the original.

Arguing from these questionings, it could be regarded as no more than logical and, moreover, consistent with historic intention, that some method other than judicial opinion should be found for constitutional change, one that did not completely disregard the preamble's claim that what followed did proceed from the people.

The body of implication, by now, taken as a whole, was an immense enlargement of the original meanings and much of it had been created by the Court; but the Court was not alone in making departures. The other branches had also distended their responsibilities. Sometimes they had reached for powers they had not possessed before; sometimes these powers had been thought necessary in emergency. Sometimes the Congress had thrust powers on the president. Then again, its members had spasmodically invaded the executive, seeking to control its operations for their own purposes. The president, being pressed by national needs, or besieged by those with claims on him, often demanded legislation. He, being the most conspicuous policy-maker, most often felt the reactions of those who were the least favored of citizens. Both legislators and presidents tended to become self-righteous about their behavior of this sort. Special pleading became the rule, but one thing always happened—offenders always appealed to the Constitution for justification. They always found in it support for whatever position they had taken.

Situations became more confused when both branches acted together to extend the government's reach. Where, in the Constitution, could justification be found for declarations of emergency? By the 1970's the states of emergency, first "limited" and then "unlimited," proclaimed by Roosevelt in 1939 and 1941, and renewed on other occasions, had been in existence for several decades, long after the war justifying them had ended. They had continued on the assumption that national interests required protection from foreign aggressions that precluded waiting for legislative approval. Perhaps this was true, but it was not contemplated by any clause of the Constitution.

This, however, like other departures, had many precedents. President John Adams had exercised such powers and had been rebuked by the Court (in *Little* vs. *Barreme* 2 Cr., 6 U.S. 170) because his executive order had exceeded an authorization by the Congress. Jefferson had better luck when he sent a naval squadron to protect American commerce from Mediterranean pirates. His action was justified in that emergency in the same terms Lincoln would later use: "To lose our country by a scrupulous adherence to written law would be to lose the law itself, with life, liberty and all those who are enjoying them with us, thus absurdly sacrificing the end to the means." When the Supreme Court had to meet the issue on somewhat different ground in 1952 (in *Youngstown Sheet & Tube Co.* v. *Sawyer,* 343 U.S. 579 [1952]), justices would write separate opinions, some defending the president's seizure of certain steel mills because of urgent need, some saying he had exceeded his powers under the existing legislation. It was impossible to learn what an emergency was considered to be, except that if it was really acute and the two branches agreed, the court might find it justifiable. All three branches in such a case would have abandoned the Constitution for an agreed imaginary one, not defined but, in their view, necessary in the public interest.

The justices may have disagreed on many occasions but they were always clear about one thing. They proposed to keep for themselves the power to say when an emergency existed and to decide if one or both of the other branches had gone further than the circumstances warranted. This was only a somewhat exaggerated instance of the method gradually gaining acceptance for enlargement. Those who approved such expanded meanings were pleased. Others were dismayed.

These last expressed their concern in such reasoning as this: Administrators of vast enterprises, not mentioned in the Constitution, were bound to look for legitimization of what they were doing. This could best be done by amendment, but if amendment was not possible it must be done by persuading the Court that justification could be found in Hamilton's rule. Instead of holding to literal constrictions, the justices were compelled to carry on a strained effort to approve necessary departures. Their procedures, however, prevented forthrightness. They merely said that what was going on was or was not allowable. What alternatives were available the justices usually did not say.

The interests whose organizations were prospering, and had escaped reproof, might prefer it this way. Their lawyers obviously would. But there was always uncertainty. This they would have to live with—assisted by counsel.

8: "Necessary and Proper"

That the "necessary and proper" clause of the Constitution would be used to do more than expand the seventeen clauses (of Article I, Section 8) preceding it was made amply clear during Washington's first administration.* One of the issues confronting the new government was whether a national bank could be established as Hamilton, then secretary of the treasury, thought it necessary to do. Washington, scanning the Constitution, could not identify any passage permitting such an enterprise by the government. As was to be his habit, he asked his associates to give him advice: Should he, or should he not, approve the bill passed by the Congress, and what would be his authority if he did approve?

Both Hamilton and Jefferson produced characteristic—and opposing—opinions. Jefferson's advice was negative. He based it on the still pending tenth amendment. His biographer, Douglas Southall Freeman, has succinctly described his position:

> The bill, Jefferson said, was manifestly unconstitutional, because congress was not vested with speci-

---

*To make all laws which shall be necessary and proper for carrying into execution the foregoing powers, and all other powers vested by this constitution in the government of the United States, or in any department or officer thereof.

> fic authority to create such a corporation, and
> under the amendment then in process of adoption
> "the powers not delegated to the United States by
> the constitution, nor prohibited by it to the states
> are reserved to the states respectively, or to the
> people."*

Jefferson's reply was made in January of 1791; the
tenth amendment on which it was premised, did not
come into force until almost a year later, but he was
certain that it would and that it expressed a necessary
principle. He considered that it would preclude all activities not originally mentioned in the Constitution or
included in it by amendment; that was what was meant
by reserving all other powers "to the states or to the
people." "States," he thought, referred to the state
legislatures. He regarded it as an absolute prohibition of
expansion by implication.

Since the amendment was not yet in effect, Washington did not have to decide on its applicability, but he
did have to decide whether an agency not mentioned in
the Constitution could be justified by reasonable extension of the powers it granted.

Madison, although not a member of the cabinet (he
was at that time serving in the House of Representatives), was respected by Washington for his knowledge
and experience. He was also asked for an opinion. He
wrote:

> I object to the bill because it is an essential princi-
> ple of the government that powers not delegated
> by the constitution cannot be rightfully exercised;
> because the power proposed by the bill to be

*In *George Washington*, 7 vols. (New York: Scribner's, 1954),
6:292.

> exercised is not delegated; and because I cannot
> satisfy myself that it results from any expressed
> power *by fair and safe rules* of implication [empha-
> ses added].*

It was not indicated where "fair and safe rules" could be
found. Madison's earlier avoidance of the term "implication" made its employment here surprising. It must be
interpreted as a concession to the argument of the broad
constructionists, and Jefferson cannot have liked this
apostasy of his most faithful disciple. By granting the
possible validity of implication, an immense variety of
powers could be called "necessary and proper." Madison
had certainly been aware of this in 1788 during the
Virginia ratification discussions. At that time he was
attempting to refute Patrick Henry's contention that
dangerous expansions did indeed lurk behind the proposed constitution. He did not admit that any such
possibility existed. Four years later, however, he was
conceding—or feeling it safe to recognize—that "fair and
safe rules" might guide necessary enlargements of a too
constricting document.

Hamilton, who responded to Washington's request
with a 15,000 word treatise, offered the following sum-
mation:

> ... this general principle is inherent in the very
> definition of government, and essential to every
> step of the progress to be made by that of the
> United States, namely: That every power vested in
> a government is in its nature sovereign, and in-
> cludes, by force of the term, a right to employ all
> the means requisite and fairly applicable to the
> attainment of the ends by such power, and which

*Freeman, ibid., 6: 292.

are not precluded by restrictions and exceptions specified in the constitution, or not immoral, or not contrary to the essential ends of political society.*

This argument was consistent with those he had made in *The Federalist* and elsewhere. What makes it problematic is its avoidance of any statement designating the powers vested in the government; that is, his argument relied on the ability to identify precisely what powers the government did possess. Lacking that, the permissible means for attaining them were too vague to be convincing. Actually the greater part of the controversy over ratification had centered in what authority the new government was being granted. Thus, even given Hamilton's argument that a power specified must include the means "applicable to the attainment of the ends of such power," it still was not indicated what those ends might be. The Bank Act of 1791 was most certainly an early test of the doctrine of implication, and Washington's signature greatly assisted in its acceptance as a method of expansion. Jefferson's disagreement had not convinced the president, nor had Madison's opinion that it did not come within fair and safe rules.

Not only was the doctrine thus affirmed by Washington but its double application was established as well. It was one thing to conclude, as was done on Hamilton's advice, that the government had powers not made explicit in the Constitution; it was quite another to conclude that the assigning of powers *within* the government could also be determined by implication. Fair and safe rules were themselves subject to interpretation, but whatever they were they now applied both to the divi-

*Freeman, ibid., 6:293.

sion of powers between the federal and state governments and among the branches of the federal government.
The Constitution was expansible or it was not.

The arrangement for divisions among the three
branches suggested to those of Federalist persuasion
that rules need not be formulated. When the Constitution omitted directives, as it did about the organization
of departments and the dismissal of their officers, the
omissions could be filled in by whatever arrangement
contestants might ultimately agree on—rather than by
any constitutional rule.

So we see that at the very beginning of the government's operations the Constitution began to unfold. The
practical arrangements for cooperation, or, at least, mutual tolerance between the Congress and the president,
arrived at in Washington's time, would be followed by
ones of considerably greater consequence, but it was in
these earliest years that the compromising began and the
Constitution began to soften and lose its sharp outlines.

By the beginning of Jefferson's presidency in 1800 it
was accepted generally that the federal government
might use the "necessary and proper" clause to expand
its activities beyond those mentioned in the Constitution. It had already done so. But it was not known how
far beyond the specified directives the president could
go in the exercise of executive powers, or to what
extent the Congress could interfere in administrative
matters. Arrangements in all such matters were, as they
had been from the first, arrived at by bargaining. Once
strict construction was abandoned, the limits of implication depended on what powers could be seized and
kept. It was not yet publicly known that Jefferson had
opposed broad construction when asked for advice by
Washington; his memorandum on the establishment of

the bank had not been made public; and now that he was president his adherence to it could be tested without the embarrassment of his former commitment.

He was president for eight years and during that time his political domination of the Congress was so complete that whatever differences they had were settled without disturbance. He found occasions when both government expansiveness and executive initiative seemed necessary. He committed the government to actions beyond its stated powers and, moreover, did things he should not have done without prior congressional approval—if he held to his own principles. Privately, as we have seen, he admitted as much.

His most notorious departure was in his handling of the Louisiana purchase. This involved the use of implied powers both for the government and for himself as president. His representation to the Congress, while negotiations were going on, was that only the island of New Orleans and lands east of the Mississippi were to be acquired from the French. He was surprised to hear that the whole of the Louisiana Territory might be involved, and constitutionality came to mind. The affair was complicated by the slowness, at that time, of communications both with the negotiators in Paris (his special envoy James Monroe and the resident ambassador, Robert Livingston) and with the authorities in New Orleans. The fact was that the French were in the process of taking the territory from Spain, and the transfer had not yet been completed. There were months when Jefferson and Secretary of State Madison did not know precisely what the situation was. It was necessary to give everyone involved flexible instructions, but as soon as it became known that Bonaparte wanted to sell the whole of his forthcoming acquisition, Jefferson determined to seize the opportunity. He knew that an immense area was involved, perhaps larger than the then United States itself, but neither he nor anyone else knew where the boundaries were and, consequently, what was being acquired.

He was quite aware that there was no warrant in the Constitution for the annexation of territory. To assume that it might be done was a wider departure than the establishment of the national bank he had so emphatically disapproved. He was disturbed. In a letter in August of 1803 he said plainly: "The general government has no power but such as the constitution has given it; and it has not given it a power of holding foreign territory, and still less of incorporating it into the union."*

In another letter (to Senator Breckenridge of Kentucky) he described his dilemma:

> The Executive in seizing the fugitive occurrence which so much advances the good of the country have done an act beyond the constitution. The legislature in casting behind them metaphysical subtleties, and risking themselves like faithful servants, must ratify and pay for it, and throw themselves on their country for doing for them unauthorized what we know they would have done for themselves had they been in a situation to do it.

He continued to be tormented all during the progress of the negotiations by doubts about the stretching of powers. His compunction was revealed to several cor-

---

*Jefferson to John Dickinson, quoted in Dumas Malone, *Jefferson the President: First Term, 1801–1805* (Boston: Little, Brown, 1970), p. 313. The quotations immediately following are also to be found in Malone.

respondents. He said, in answering a letter from Senator Nicholas of Virginia, who had urged him not to admit publicly that he doubted the legitimacy of what was being done:

> When an instrument admits two constructions, the one safe, the other dangerous, the one precise, the other indefinite, I prefer that which is safe and precise. I had rather ask an enlargement of power from the nation where it is found necessary, than to assume it by a construction which would make our powers boundless. Our peculiar security is in possession of a written constitution. Let us not make it a blank paper by construction. I say the same as to the opinion of those who consider the grant of the treaty-making power as boundless. If it is then we have no constitution. . . . Let us go on then perfecting it, by adding by way of amendment, those powers which time and trial show are still wanting. . . .

Nevertheless, he yielded to the advice of friends who warned him about the political danger of admitting doubts. He drafted at least two amendments and consulted with Madison and others about the advisability of asking the Congress to accept them, but finally put them aside. He wrote to Nicholas:

> I confess that I think it important in the present case to set an example against broad construction by appealing for new power to the people. If, however, our friends shall think differently, certainly I shall acquiesce with satisfaction, confiding that the good sense of our country will correct the evil construction when it shall produce ill effects.

This concession of Jefferson, together with "the compromise of 1789"—both extraconstitutional arrangements—must be taken to show that in these early administrations there was firmly fixed the precedent for the expansions of later years, both as to what powers the government could assume and what the president could do when the prospect of danger or advantage required it.

This last was not quite the full-blown "doctrine of necessity" it became when the nation's security was threatened; that waited until Lincoln met the challenge of the secessionists by expending funds without congressional approval and suspending the writ of habeas corpus. These, and others of Lincoln's actions, were undertaken in an emergency whose demands were beyond any grants to be found in the Constitution. He accepted the responsibility and made no public apology for it. He told the Congress (on July 4, 1861), when he asked for ratification of measures he had already taken, that he had moved to meet the challenge of rebellion, "using means, which, whether strictly legal or not, were ventured upon under what appeared to be public demand, and a public necessity; trusting then as now that congress would readily ratify them." His final word was this:

> I felt that measures, otherwise unconstitutional, might become lawful by becoming indispensable to the preservation of the constitution through the preservation of the nation.

Between Jefferson and Lincoln there had been Jackson, a fierce protector of presidential prerogatives. On several occasions he reminded opponents that only the president represented all the people and that this gave him both duties and powers no other official possessed. By his time, too, the expansion of the nation had begun to test the limits of numerous assumptions. That the government would have many new responsibilities was obvious and the Constitution must not stand in the way. It must be made flexible for the enlarging needs, and since amendment was difficult if not impossible it must be held that anything not prohibited could be done. Implication was already an accepted means of expansion. In time departures from original and literal meanings would on occasion be justified by reasoning so strained as hardly to be credible. Its conclusions, moreover, were subject to reversal. The axiom that one Congress may not commit its successors applied as well to the Supreme Court.

9: Foreign Policy:
Presidential Primacy

It may be as well for an understanding of the president's leadership in the making of foreign policy to begin with a recital of the Constitution's actual directive. It is to be found in Section 2 of Article II:

> He shall have the power, by and with the advice and consent of the senate, to make treaties, provided two-thirds of the senators present concur; and he shall nominate, and by and with the advice and consent of the senate, shall appoint ambassadors, other public ministers and consuls. . . .

This states clearly enough that the Framers meant the making of treaties to be done with the *advice* as well as the *consent* of the Senate. Washington, meaning to be a good president, and having a literal mind, sought to consult the Senate on the first occasion when it was required. This was in 1791. There were treaties to be made with Indians on the northwest borders and difficulties were arising not only from opposition to the persistent movement of settlers into new territory but from the continuing assistance being given the Indians by the British in violation of postwar agreements. Although this was an extremely important question for the future, he was put off by the senators. They refused to discuss the matter in his presence. He was told that his papers would be referred to a committee for study and that he would be told the result. He was annoyed, and when he thought it over, considered that the humiliation was one he would not risk another time. Treaties would be submitted for consent only after their completion. Advice during negotiation would no longer be sought.

The constitutional question arose again, and in even more exigent circumstances, when Washington was compelled to decide whether the nation should allow itself to be involved in European war. On April 22, 1793, he issued a proclamation of neutrality. As usual, he was cautious about going beyond what were clearly his responsibilities and the words used had to be carefully chosen.

The contingency was such that presidential action seemed to him the only way to escape a dangerous involvement; the French had declared war on Britain and they were linked to the United States by treaties negotiated just after the peace in 1788, but the British had become important trading partners and to begin hostilities with them would have been costly, perhaps fatal. To take a position on either side would have been a commitment to something the young nation could not afford. There were hundreds of American ships at sea and the British were still holding forts on the northwest borders and supporting the Indians in opposition to advancing settlers.

One of the existing treaties with the French had to do with friendship and commerce, but the other required active collaboration with them in protecting their Caribbean colonies, and this would be a taking of sides. Responsibility under the treaties, however, was not Washington's only concern. What was causing the immediate crisis was public enthusiasm for the French revolution. It was reaching hysterical proportions, and the mobs in Philadelphia's streets were shouting for war. To them the cause was one of liberty against royal oppression. In spite of Washington's efforts to remain above what he called faction, he was being denounced as a Federalist and all Federalists were identified by the Republicans as monarchists.

The situation became intolerable when Edmond Genet, ambassador from the new government in France, reached the United States. It soon became plain that his mission was to excite such support for the revolutionary cause that Americans would be persuaded to take sides. He landed at Charleston early in the spring of 1793, just after the beginning of Washington's second term. It happened that the president, after inauguration, had gone to Mount Vernon on urgent business having to do with the management of his estate, but soon after his arrival a letter from Hamilton told him that France, already at war with Austria and Prussia, had now declared war on Holland, Spain, and Britain. He left his private concerns and hurried back to Philadelphia where he was appalled to hear of Genet's exciting of fervor for intervention. Americans were being divided as they had not been divided since the rebellion. Federalists regarded Genet's behavior as an outrageous violation of protocol. Before he had left Charleston he had commissioned several privateers and had set up a court to award captured British ships as prizes. These were inadmissible violations of American sovereignty. Then, on his way north, he had made speeches wherever a crowd could be gathered. When he finally reached Philadelphia and presented himself as ambassador he plainly expected to be received as a popular hero. Instead Washington accorded him a frosty official reception. Being annoyed by this

and encouraged by his supporters, he publicly threatened an appeal to the people against the president. This
impudence on the part of a foreigner infuriated Washington, but he refused to lose sight of the nation's clear
interest in neutrality. He waited for the answers to
several questions he had submitted to his advisers.

These questions had to do not only with the status of
the French treaties but with the consequences if the
United States should be drawn into the conflict on
either side. Beyond this he wanted opinions about his
own responsibility in formulating policy. Genet's agitation and the popular response made it necessary to have
answers immediately. Something approaching civil war
seemed imminent.

Were the treaties in effect after the overthrow of the
royal government in France? They had been made in the
name of Louis XVI, who had been deposed. Hamilton
thought the revolution had cancelled them. Jefferson
held that the agreements had been made with the
French nation, not with a particular government. Knox
agreed with Hamilton. Randolph felt that since there
was no other way of establishing neutrality a presidential proclamation was imperative regardless of the treaties and of public clamor for intervention.

Because Washington was still trying to hold both
Republicans, represented by Jefferson, and Federalists,
represented by Hamilton, in his cabinet, he sought to
soften the refusal of intervention favored by Jefferson
but also to make it clear that this did not mean active
support for the British. He asked Randolph, as the most
moderate of his group, to draft a proclamation.

All agreed after discussion that Washington must
make a statement. Jefferson, however, thought such a
proclamation would be nothing less than a declaration

that there should be no war and, he said, the Congress alone had the power to decide for war or peace. He also put forward the practical objection that it would be better to hold back any declaration of neutrality. It would be worth something to the powers at war, and both might bid for American support. The broadest privileges of a neutral nation might be demanded as a price.

Washington was impressed and was also worried about exceeding his powers, but he still felt forced by the increasing furor in the streets to take a firm stand for neutrality. By now numerous groups called Democratic Societies were being formed. These were suspiciously similar to the effective committees of correspondence in the years preceding the American rebellion. Altogether the shouting for liberty and for joining with the French revolutionaries in their fight against royalist oppressors made the situation increasingly perilous.

The decision, after the conferring on April 19 among his advisers, was that Randolph's draft should omit the word "neutrality," now charged with such emotion. There should, instead, be an affirmation of friendly concern for both the French and the British peoples. Also it was to be understood that the Congress, in its next session, should not be bound by the proclamation.

When the proclamation was made public on April 22 there was the expected uproar in the city. Threats were made to drag Washington from his house and compel his consent to support of the revolution. For a few days Federalists were mostly in hiding and the president besieged, but he refused to show the least concern, and gradually the crowds quieted. Genet's diatribes drew smaller and smaller crowds and the city went back to its domestic concerns.

Of all those who commented on all this, Madison seems to have been alone in making the constitutional issue his first concern. He was, of course, a member of the House, and, since the next session would not begin until the following December, he was not in Philadelphia. But Jefferson wrote to him, admitting that he had agreed finally with the decision to maintain neutrality and to have the president issue a statement of public policy. He recognized that the young nation could not afford a war, but he was still troubled about the presidential prerogative. Two letters written in reply (one on May 8 and one on June 19) stated more clearly than Jefferson had done the Republican position. It was, indeed, a kind of rebuke.

The first letter described the proclamation as:

> ... a most unfortunate error. It wounds the national honor by seeming to disregard the stipulated duties to France. It wounds the popular feelings by seeming indifference to the cause of liberty. And it seems to violate the form and spirit of the constitution by making the Executive Magistrate the organ ... of the nation in relation to war and peace. ...

The second letter went on to state the strict construction doctrine as applied to presidential conduct:

> I am extremely afraid that the president may not be sufficiently aware of the snares that may be laid for his good intentions by the men whose politics at bottom are very different from his own. An assumption of prerogatives not clearly found in the constitution and having the appearance of being

copied from a monarchical model will beget animadversion equally mortifying to him and disadvantageous to the government.*

When the Congress met nine months later a neutrality act was passed, thus giving legislative support to the policy of the proclamation. This seemed to justify the president's enlargement of his constitutional directive. It also established him permanently as the negotiator of treaties and as the shaper of foreign policy. E. S. Corwin has related this to a wider issue—that of the Senate acting as must have been contemplated by the word "advise." Said Corwin:

> ... the senate's function as an executive council was, from the very beginning put, and very largely by its own election, on the way to absorption into its more usual function as a legislative chamber, and subsequently development soon placed its decision in this respect beyond possibility of recall.**

The same assumption was made in the constitutional compendium issued as a Senate document in 1964.***

Louis Fisher does not agree. He advises caution in accepting such a flat statement. Referring to the difficulty Washington had with the Senate concerning the Indian treaty he puts it this way:

> The lesson to be drawn from this episode is not that the president, from that time forward, re-

---

*These letters are to be found in the final volume of the Douglas Southall Freeman biography *George Washington,* 7 vols. (seventh volume by J. A. Carroll and Mary Wells Ashworth [New York: Scribners, 1957]), 7:53.

**The President: Office and Powers,* 4th ed. (New York: New York University Press, 1957).

***The Constitution of the United States of America: Analysis and Interpretation,* 88th Cong., 1 Session, 463.

garded the negotiation of treaties as a purely executive matter, or that the role of the senate was thenceforth limited to voting up or down a treaty which the administration had formulated and drafted. And yet this impression has been promoted by Professor Corwin. . . . Washington's experience merely ended the possibility of *personal consultation*. Joint negotiations continued, not by personal consultation but rather by written communication.*

It is not necessary for the purpose here to distinguish Corwin's view from that of Fisher. Whether or not Washington's successors would consider themselves authorized to conduct foreign policy as they conceived it ought to be conducted, that is what they most certainly did. None of them would feel it necessary to do more than consult a few senators informally about even the most important initiatives. Sometimes this turned out well, as when Jefferson arranged for the Louisiana purchase; sometimes it turned out badly, as when Wilson was refused consent to the Treaty of Versailles. But it has been the rule.

This is a curious constitutional development. Usually implied enlargements have had their origin in ambiguous directives. The rule has seemed to stem from Hamilton's argument that a power conferred carried with it the means necessary for its implementation, but the presidential primacy in foreign policy came about in another way—by dropping from consideration an embarrassing directive and thereafter ignoring it. This directive is so categorical, and certain incidents of presidential behavior in shaping foreign relations have been so annoying,

*_The President and Congress_ (New York: Free Press, 1972), p. 43.

that from time to time senators have called attention to their lost constitutional powers and have tried to effect their recovery.* Nothing however, has come of these efforts.

Here, again, what seems to be most important is the neglect of amendment. The directive to seek advice still remained in the Constitution, although as a reality it had ceased to exist in the first instance of an attempt to make use of it. Presidential primacy was simply extrapolated from one of two equally clear words. The inconvenient one was ignored. Whether the Senate ought to involve itself in the preliminaries of treaty-making is a question that was never really settled. It could only be finally settled by amendment. Because it has not, presidents are periodically attacked for acting without consultation, but although they have sometimes been rebuked by rejection of their efforts, they have continued to negotiate without substantial senatorial participation. The "advice" of the Constitution has been ignored.

In a situation of this kind there is no recourse. Senators cannot sue for a restoration of rights. They cannot make treaties on their own. They can turn balky and refuse the consent necessary to ratification; but presidents cannot be compelled to include them in negotiations.

*In 1973 Senator Hartke introduced a resolution "designed to restore the senate to its rightful constitutional place in the treaty-making process . . ." There have been many such protests.

10: Judicial Supremacy:
Marbury vs. *Madison*

It is generally assumed that it was Chief Justice Marshall who established the doctrine of judicial supremacy. Actually, however, his declaration in 1803 that acts of the legislature could be rejected if the justices should find them in conflict with the constitution, was not the first. An earlier case, *Hylton* vs. *U.S.* (3 Dall. 171 [1796, 234]) carried a similar affirmation.

The specific question was whether the Congress, in taxing carriages, had imposed a direct tax or an excise. A direct tax would conflict with the provision of the Constitution requiring that these should be apportioned among the states according to population. The Court held that only land taxes and capitations (head taxes) were direct. The carriage tax was an excise and therefore constitutional.

The open presumption, although the law was upheld, was that the interpretation of the Constitution was to be the responsibility of the Court. By 1803, when *Marbury* vs. *Madison* was decided, most federal judges and most lawyers assumed that the Court had this power. When Marshall seized the opportunity to affirm the principle in a much publicized case his decision turned interpretation once for all into determination. That the opinion was a rebuke to Jefferson, who held the opposite view, made it a political issue.

The situation was peculiar and there was already a history of controversy. It will be recalled that Jefferson relied on the tenth amendment (not yet ratified) in his advice to Washington about the signing of Hamilton's bill establishing a national bank. Marshall in effect nullified this amendment by reversing Jefferson's reading of its meaning. Jefferson, of course, was president when *Marbury* vs. *Madison* was decided in 1803.*

To understand how Marshall, as chief justice of a court not at all highly regarded in those times, could have fixed, so clearly and so finally the course of legal history, it is necessary to know something about the circumstances enabling this remarkable man to determine the position of the Constitution—or the Court's conception of it—in American polity.

He had been one of the Virginia lawyers who had been leaders in the rebellion and later in the new government. Before he had become a member of the profession, he had been one of Washington's soldiers, and had served throughout the war. He was self-educated in the law, except that for a few months he had attended the lectures of George Wythe, the teacher of so many who had helped to create the Republic. He was licensed in 1780; from then until he was persuaded by President Adams to become, first, chief justice, then, in the last month of that unhappy president's administration, secretary of state as well, he refused all invitations to enter public service except as a legislator in Virginia. He had been too young to be a delegate to the Convention in 1787 but during the next year he had been one of the most effective proponents of ratification—along with Madison—in the Virginia convention.

Marbury vs. *Madison* (1 Cr. 137).

The Supreme Court needed a strong and talented guide after its listless beginning and Marshall supplied a leadership that was to last for 35 years. If it seems strange that a chief justice should concurrently be secretary of state, it has to be remembered that the early court had few cases and that his secretaryship was only a last-minute service to a fading Federalist president.

Jefferson came from the same Virginia group. He also came from the same upland environment. Both made their own way into the legal profession and public life, in spite of having heavy family responsibilities and no family wealth for backing. Jefferson was 12 years Marshall's senior and had been precocious enough to have been entrusted with drafting the Declaration of Independence when he was only 33. Jefferson's experience also had been different. He had spent years in France as an American emissary, and, although he was a landed proprietor, was deeply persuaded that the cause of the common people ought to prevail. He hoped for a nation of small-holders owing little to government and expecting little from it.

Marshall, on the contrary, was a convinced unionist and this, as national political parties were formed, meant that he was a Federalist, along with Washington, Hamilton, Adams, and others of those who had largely dominated the Philadelphia convention. Jefferson did not recognize the younger man's formidable talents until too late and then could find no way of countering his initiative within the canons of respect for public amenities.

The decision concerning Marbury's petition was made in a situation that seems not at all likely to have generated one of the most consequential opinions ever issued by the Court. As has been noted, the Constitution from the first had been the subject of controversy between the strict and loose constructionists, Jefferson being the most determined of those who insisted on literalism and Hamilton the proponent of free interpretation. For the Jeffersonians the question had been—as Madison said— what were "fair and safe rules" for expansion, and these were conceived to be few and restrictive. It remained for Marshall to make use of "fair and safe" in a way no Democratic-Republican would have approved.

He did this in what historians are apt to speak of as "the cleverest legal-political maneuver" in American history, the cleverness consisting of finding a way to prevent Jefferson from making any protest. What had raised the issue was that Adams, after being defeated and before leaving office, had done what he could to perpetuate Federalist principles now that the Jeffersonians were to take over the government. He was certain of their intention to undo all his own and Washington's efforts to strengthen the national union. Only the judiciary, being appointed for life, might resist successfully. That branch, at least, might be fortified against the disunionists. It was for this that he appointed Marshall to the chief justiceship and made other last-minute Federalist appointments. These included a number of new justices of the peace for the District of Columbia. Some commissions for these officers had been signed but not delivered when Jefferson was inaugurated. When he discovered this he ordered Madison, his new secretary of state, not to deliver them. Four of these appointees, led by William Marbury, petitioned the Supreme Court for a writ of mandamus to compel their issuance. Madison ignored a preliminary order signed by Marshall, and just then the Congress stopped all operations of the Court for more than a year to keep it from deciding whether on appeal the judiciary act of 1801 was valid. Consequently Marbury's petition could not be acted on until 1803 when proceedings were resumed.

Marshall had, it seemed, two alternatives. He could order Madison to make the delivery, knowing that Jefferson would not allow Madison to comply, or back down and not issue the writ. Either would admit the Court's impotence. The resourceful chief justice, however, found a third way, one that resulted in a claim to far vaster power than Marbury had requested the Court to use. It was also an alternative that allowed Jefferson to block Marbury from gaining the office he sought—and so precluded a protest.

The third way was this: the Marbury petition had been made in accordance with the judiciary act of 1789, providing that the Supreme Court should have "power to issue writs of mandamus, in cases warranted by the principles and usages of law, to any courts appointed, or persons holding office, under the authority of the United States." Marbury had applied directly to the Supreme Court rather than first to a lower court. The Constitution (in Article II), however, provided that the Supreme Court should have original jurisdiction only when ambassadors, ministers, and consuls were affected and Marbury had been appointed to none of these offices. The statute therefore, Marshall said, went beyond the constitutional definition of judicial authority. The Congress had attempted to expand the Court's jurisdiction and this it had no power to do.

Historians have pointed out since that such a holding was "preposterous." The statute had been interpreted before in such a way as to raise no such question.* Nevertheless Marshall, asking first in his opinion whether Marbury was entitled to the commission, said that he was and that it had been illegally withheld. Then he asked whether the laws of the country afforded a remedy. He said that they did. But then he went on to the jurisdictional question: had Marbury applied for a remedy he was entitled to? Only then did he announce the discovery of a conflict between section 13 of the judiciary act and Article III of the Constitution. This brought him to the statement that has been regarded ever since as the authority for judicial review:

> If a law be in opposition to the constitution, if both the law and the constitution apply to a particular case, so that the court must either find it conformable to the law, disregarding the constitution, or conformable to the constitution, disregarding the law, the court must determine which of these conflicting rules governs the case, that is of the very essence of judicial duty.

Since this also allowed the Court to say what the Constitution meant, it became the accepted official statement of the doctrine of implication. The Constitution had not said that the Court could make any such determination, but now, by inference, it claimed that privilege. It thus joined the Congress and the executive in expanding its own powers. It might, of course, as they might, encounter opposition from the other branches. Then there might be a confrontation if neither opponent gave way.

The difference between the Court's claim to expan-

*C. H. Pritchett, *The American Constitution*, 2nd ed. (New York: McGraw-Hill, 1968), p. 164.

sion and that of the other branches was that it also claimed the right to determine the limits of *their* expansion. The claim would never afterward be successfully challenged.*

*For a recent account of Marshall's life and work the reader is referred to *John Marshall: A Life in Law* by Leonard Baker (New York: Macmillan, 1974).

11: National Supremacy:
McCulloch vs. *Maryland*

The conclusion reached by Marshall in *Marbury* would have been astonishing to the Framers, and most of them would have repudiated any intention to have the Court assume to be the arbiter of disputes and the allocator of power within the government. It must be said, however, that it was the result of the Framers' own unwillingness to arrange for future changes in an effective way. There had to be accommodations; they had provided no other way than amendment; and amendment had almost at once proved to be impractical by the methods they had settled on.

Marbury has been described. The *McCulloch* case (4 Wheat. 316) involved an issue more important than potential quarrels between the branches, and more important, even, than the claim of the judiciary to be the arbiter of those powers. This was the ascendancy of the national government itself in any dispute with the states.

The theory of concurrent sovereignty had been agreed to in the wrangling at the Convention between the nationalists and the states' righters. Part of the concession yielded by the nationalists was equal representation for both large and small states in a second legislative house. Not fully satisfied with this, the states' righters demanded a clause guaranteeing that the arrangement would never be changed. Nevertheless, concurrent sovereignty remained a delicate matter, an unstable division, bound from the outset to be looked at differently by nationalists and localists. It was the basis for the party division, not recognized by the Framers, but existent in latent form as they confronted each other on numerous other issues. Again, in Washington's administration, it was the cause of repeated confrontations between Jefferson and Hamilton, and later it would divide Lincoln from his opponents—Democrats (as they would be then).

McCulloch, however, was decided in 1819, four decades before the Civil War. A state was, for the first time, directly challenging federal authority. The issue involved the same national bank that had elicited the opposing memoranda of Jefferson and Hamilton in 1791. Washington having accepted Hamilton's argument, the bank had been in existence some twenty-eight years. It had become extremely unpopular. It had failed to assure financial stability and had done nothing to check the speculative boom that just then was ending in a collapse marked by numerous failures of businesses and banks. There was, indeed, full scale depression, with the usual unemployment and distress among debtors. Some of the bank's branches had been deeply involved in speculation and were known to have engaged in fraudulent practices. What usefulness it may have had was undermined and its enemies were numerous and active.

The Maryland legislature was responding to widespread indignation when it imposed a heavy tax on the Baltimore branch of the bank. Maryland was not the only state to do this. Similar laws were passed throughout the south and west, with an especially drastic one in

Ohio. The Baltimore action was challenged by the bank. The chief justice, in writing the opinion for the Court seemed never to have heard the critics, and he carried with him the unanimous support of his associates as he pursued the familiar nationalist logic.

It had to be decided first whether the government had the power to establish such a bank, a matter that, in spite of the controversy over its founding, had never come before the Court. The case was argued by the best-known lawyers in the country, including Daniel Webster and William Pinckney for the bank and Luther Martin and Joseph Hopkinson for Maryland. It took Marshall only three days to hand down a decision. He held that such a bank could be chartered by the national government, that this power was exclusive, and that a state could not interfere with an agency of that government by taxing it. The state law, he held flatly, was unconstitutional.

His opinion pointed out that the authority of the federal government came directly from the people rather than from the states as entities. He admitted that sovereignty was divided between the nation and the states, and that the states did retain a sphere of authority, but the national government, he said, "though limited in its powers, is supreme within its sphere of action." It remained only to define that sphere of action.

It had to be admitted that establishing a bank was not among the enumerated powers of the Congress, but there were also implied powers. These, Marshall argued, had two sources. The legislature, for one thing, must by its very nature be able to select the means for putting its directives into effect; also there was the "necessary and proper" clause of the Constitution. This, he said, did not mean that the methods chosen had to be absolutely indispensable. There were obviously degrees of necessity. As to the test for determining the constitutionality of any implied power:

> We must never forget that it is a constitution we are expounding . . . Let the end be legitimate, let it be within the scope of the constitution, and all means which are appropriate, which are plainly adapted to that end, which are not prohibited, but consist with the letter and spirit of the constitution, are constitutional.

It will be seen that these words followed closely Hamilton's original statement of the implication doctrine. They were now formalized by the Court. Marshall was blunt and conclusive. Since the bank was a lawful agency of the government, the act establishing it must prevail against any attempt of a state to limit or control its action. He cited the "supremacy clause." The Constitution, treaties, and acts of the Congress were the supreme law of the land and must be respected. He went on to say that "the power to tax was the power to destroy." If federal agencies could be taxed by the states their continued existence would be dependent on the states' consent, and this was a wholly inadmissable conclusion: "The American people did not design their government to be dependent on the states."

The decision had immediate repercussions. It was printed everywhere and those on either side were voluble and angry in their support or condemnation. The denunciations were especially bitter among the distressed debtors. Objectors said that efforts to get rid of the hated bank were being frustrated by a few men who were beyond the reach of electoral reprimand. The Court thus shared popular displeasure with the bank.

Strong resentment was expressed through the Midwest, but there was even more radical reaction in the deep south where already the forces were gathering for renewed battles over states' rights. These, as it happened, were exacerbated by the extension of slavery into the western territories. The protest made itself felt in newspaper diatribes, in public meetings, and, in Virginia, by an immediate protest by judges of the court of appeals supported by both Jefferson and Madison.

There followed at once a movement for constitutional amendment meant to redefine the division of powers between the state and federal governments. Most state legislatures considered the question. Five formally petitioned the Congress to call a convention, but nine refused. The movement came gradually to an end, demonstrating again that amendment was to be avoided in settling constitutional questions. Another conclusion to be drawn from the furor over *McCulloch* was that the national government, whenever its power was asserted, was to be supreme. Still another was that the Court would expect to decide where the lines of concurrent sovereignty were to be drawn.

It seems strange that in such troubled years, issues of national importance were not referred to the people for decision but were to end in opinions rendered by a majority of the justices. The Jefferson succession—in the person now of Monroe—still occupied the White House in 1819. His years had come to be known as the "era of good feelings," because of the temporary quieting of so many old controversies, but actually the slavery issue still festered, especially in the border states. What was later called the Missouri Compromise left dangerous antagonisms. Also this "good feelings" ascription was dubious for another reason. The really terrible depression following years of speculation had hurt most citizens badly. It seems strange to a later generation, used to political responsibility for economic affairs, that the president was immune from blame, but then, and for years afterward, presidents remained serenely aloof while the economy repeatedly boomed and then collapsed.

Such blame as the government bore for economic disturbance affected mostly members of the Congress until Jackson came on the scene. Then the accumulated hatred of the bank found a champion and it was presently abolished, but it was not done by state intrusion on national affairs. The court's long defense of national sovereignty with Marshall's leadership was so well established that even when he was gone the nationalists still prevailed.

The question was never settled. The Court had spoken, but dissent, especially in the South, was not extinguished. Its final emergence in outright secession would be as much because the Court had been intransigent, and completely indifferent to popular indignation, as because Lincoln refused to give way. He became the personification of unionist theory. When the Court, after its long defense of federal power, found itself led by Chief Justice Taney, who had states' rights views, the defense passed to the president. He could use force when words failed. Marshall had frustrated Jefferson. Taney could not frustrate Lincoln. He tried, but his failure was total. It was the end of Jeffersonianism. But the Constitution, as originally adopted, was hardly affected at all. Even the amendments resulting from the war, ratified without the rebellious states' consent, did not affect its structure. Moreover the Court remained, when it recovered from Taney, the final arbiter. Both judicial supremacy and national supremacy rested entirely on the theory of implication as made official by the Court. The justices had relieved the people of responsibility for their Constitution.

12: Conflict

It has been noted that, when asked about the proposal for a national bank, Jefferson supported his democratic views with the words of a prospective tenth amendment:

> The powers not delegated to the United States by the Constitution, nor prohibited by it to the states are reserved to the states respectively, or to the people.

It has been noted also that Marshall quoted the "necessary and proper" clause:

> The Congress shall have the power to make all laws which shall be necessary and proper for carrying into execution the foregoing powers and all other powers vested by this constitution in the government of the United States, or in any department or officer thereof.

Also, what was later called the "supremacy" clause:

> This constitution, and the laws of the United States which shall be made in pursuance thereof; and all treaties made, or which shall be made, under the authority of the United States, shall be the supreme law of the land and the judges in every state shall be bound thereby, anything in the con-

stitution or laws of any state to the contrary notwithstanding.

All these were certainly authentic sections of the Constitution (although the tenth amendment had arrived there a few years late); yet it is quite impossible to reconcile their opposed meanings. The tenth amendment restricts national powers to those specifically delegated to the United States or prohibited to the states. All other powers are reserved, it says firmly, to the states or to the people—that is, to agencies and officers of the states or to their electorates. The original clauses, however, affirm the supremacy of federal power in disputed areas—the principle announced by Marshall.

Since this tenth amendment was not ratified until a year after Jefferson had written his memorandum for Washington on the bank bill, and since Jefferson meanwhile had command of a formidable political machine, managed, in the Congress, by his satellite Madison, it is a fair conclusion that this addition was Jefferson's attempt to restrict the governance of the Constitution. He had been abroad in 1787, and had had no part in the Convention's deliberations, although, of course, he had had extensive correspondence with Madison for years. The finished product ran counter to his hope that the Constitution would assist in ensuring that the nation would remain one of small holders and artisans and that most of them could remain independent, self-sufficient, and largely self-governing. In his view, the central government should have been restricted to the maintenance of security and to the regulation of commerce among the states. For these duties no considerable bureaucracy would be required and there would be almost no taxes except those to support the activities of local governments. There would be no expansion by implication. That is what the tenth amendment plainly says, any loosening or expansion would have to come by way of state-wide initiations, possibly using conventions of specially elected delegates as had been the original procedure.

When he and Madison, controlling a majority, persuaded the Congress to propose the tenth amendment he could be quite certain of its ratification by three-quarters of the state legislatures. He could count on the local politicians who had lost to the nationalists at the constitutional convention; they, too, were unhappy with the Federalists' conception of nationalism. What the tenth amendment represented, then, was a repudiation of the compromise reached with so much labor and at so great a sacrifice of nationalist principles. The difficulty was that the "supremacy" and the "necessary and proper" clauses still remained in the Constitution. If these had been deleted when the tenth amendment took effect, the Constitution would have been sharply constricted and Marshall, in his exposition, would have lacked the support he depended on in *Marbury* and *McCulloch*. As it was, he could ignore the amendment, relying on clauses of the original document. So long as the Court's decrees were respected, nationalism would remain the prevailing doctrine. So would enlargement by implication.

It has been so ever since. National policy has never been held within the intention of the amendment. This is true of Court opinion as well, with the notable exception of the Taney regime which attempted to restrain the federal power and frustrate Lincoln's determination to preserve the Union. *Dred Scott* was reversed by war, and *ex parte Merriman* was a lecture addressed to a president who was not listening.* But these, too, have never been explicitly repudiated. The ambiguity has continued, generating an endless dispute between nationalists and states' righters. It might have been thought that when the post-Civil War amendments were being formulated, the tenth might have been deleted, but deletion somehow has never been accomplished. There have been additions to the original Constitution but the only subtraction has been the eighteenth (prohibition) amendment—except, of course, that the methodology of presidential elections was changed after Burr and Jefferson, under the old provision, had an embarrassingly equal number of electoral college votes. Even in that change, however, the college itself survived; it was only made impossible that such an impasse as that of 1800 should occur again.

Actually, a student trying to understand the Constitution is at times unable to conclude whether strict or loose constructions remain the controlling theory. Perhaps this is one reason why the Court has been able to remain the source of enlarged constructions when specific directives are lacking in the document itself. Americans could not continue to act on two antithetical theories at the same time. Marshall's success in repelling the Democratic-Republican attack was consolidated by the Jeffersonians' mistaken forecast of the country's future. Expansion of territory, growth of population, the intensification of technology—all these made the Jeffersonian scheme seem in a remarkably short time no more than an impossible dream. Events created an indisputable union. The Court protected it.

Dred Scott vs. *Sanford* (19 How 393); *ex parte Merriman* (17 Fed. Cases 9487).

Like others of Jefferson's schemes, that of revising the Constitution without seeming to and during the period of nationalist supremacy, was clever to the point of being sly. He could not make it effective, however, without a Court willing to choose his theory over the Hamiltonian one. He made that effort too. John Adams, in the last months of his administration, having a devastating fear of his enemies' intentions, did what he could to frustrate them by persuading the outgoing Congress to pass a new judiciary act to supersede that of 1789. The six member Court was reduced to five when the next vacancy should occur, thus giving the new president one less vacancy to fill. More district courts were created by the act and the circuit courts were abolished. Six new ones with expanded jurisdiction being substituted. The new judgeships were naturally filled by faithful Federalists. But shortly a succeeding law made the number of Supreme Court judges the same as the number of circuit courts, and as the country continued to expand, and more circuits had to be added, the Supreme Court grew larger. A seventh member was added in 1807, and, after Jefferson's time (in 1837), the number went to nine. Still later it was increased to ten. The permanent number of nine was not adopted until 1869, after some uncertainty as a result of the Civil War.

A dominating personality enabled Marshall to frustrate Jefferson's attempts to convert the Court to his political views. He apparently overawed most of his Democratic colleagues. There were some dissents, but in the great decisions of those years Marshall remained in almost undisputed control. From *Marbury* on, the Court maintained its supremacy among the branches; and, from *McCulloch* on, it supported the supremacy of the national government in disputes arising because of concurrent sovereignty—again with the exception of the Taney interlude.

There was no amendment to consolidate the Federalists' positions. There were a few attempts, but they got nowhere. This was the period of sixty years when there were no amendments at all. Why amend, it seemed to be concluded, when the Court could revise the Constitution at need?

To sum up: it was clear in 1819 that the Court had established itself with these implied powers:

1. It could declare laws passed by the Congress and signed by the president to be unconstitutional.
2. It could define the roles of the Congress and the executive in the federal system, reserving for itself a role superior to either or both.
3. It could check the expansion by implication of the other branches—unless it agreed that such expansion was "constitutional"—that the implication seemed reasonable to a majority of its members.
4. It could define the federal government's position in the system of concurrent sovereignties.
5. It could punish contempt of its decrees (a power given in the act of 1789 and never repealed) although it possessed no enforcing agency.

The difficulty with this seemingly victorious outcome of conflict among the branches was that the victories had a certain impermanency. In the American system there could be only one finality. Unless a view, a principle or a policy was embedded in the Constitution it did not have the people's imprimatur, the sine qua non of democracy. Even the Court—as had been admitted in

The Federalist—had to act in ways regarded popularly as "constitutional." If it did not there were always elections and sometimes they had the effect of rejecting Court decisions. In extreme confrontations there might be armed conflict. This would not only be true of secessionism, supported by the Court, but also of the facing up to employers by labor, for instance, and of the affluent by the needy. The Taney court was reversed; even if in a very different way, so was the reactionary one of the years before Roosevelt.

It was for this reason—uncertainty—that amendment was a necessity if the democratic system was to be made stable, not subject to the changing composition of a court majority, five appointed justices out of nine.

The Constitution, as a product of Court interpretation, became more and more ambiguous. What had begun in the nation's very first administration was relied on more as the years passed and extrapolations became more numerous. Because these were never certainly permanent, the nation found itself living with a basic law it revered but could neither understand nor depend on.

This supremacy of the Court is a peculiarity of the American system it is difficult to explain. It seems to have a very insecure place in the Constitution; it seems, indeed, to exist, as a functioning branch, at the tolerance of the Congress. Yet, as we have seen, it very early asserted its premier position and has been allowed to preserve it through the vicissitudes of nearly two centuries. Discretion has been a notable characteristic of its behavior, but more important, certainly, has been the need, in a system of interacting powers, for a place of finality, a body able to end controversy and to interpret ambiguities. It has made an imperfect Constitution tolerable. That may well account for its continued supremacy. The pretense that a body of agreed higher law exists is a kind of national conspiracy, maintained because of need. A Constitution is necessary to the American system. That it no longer exists is an intolerable thought. The Court solemnly accepts its role as the personification of constitutionalism, content to act with appropriate discretion. Generally speaking, it is allowed to do so by "the people."

13: Presidential Privilege
(According to Jefferson)

If what later was called "executive privilege" had continued to be called "presidential privilege" there would have been less trouble in understanding its place among the implied powers. Jefferson's conception of his position, at least when he began, was a good deal less expansive than that of some later presidents; nevertheless, he had a firm conviction that as an agent of the public, he must have freedom to consult and decide with no interference from anyone. It was when presidents began to consider their entire administrative establishment to be immune from inquiry and exposure that reaction began to be serious. They then came into collision with the assertions of power by the other branches.

To understand the original conception of this implied presidential immunity from interference, it is illuminating to see what happened in the trial of Aaron Burr for treason. This was the first instance of a demand for compliance with a Court order that a president felt compelled to reject. During the trial Marshall subpoenaed Jefferson—demanded his presence in Court as well as submission of all papers relevent to the charge, thus claiming competence to require obedience from the head of the executive branch. This affair did not involve the legislature as so many later ones would. It did not

109

even involve the Supreme Court as such. It arose when Marshall was the sitting judge at the district court in Richmond as Supreme Court justices were required to do under the then prevailing law. The question at issue was whether even a president must yield to the claims of a defendant for a fair trial—as defined not by the president but by a judge. Marshall rested on the assumption that executives could not be expected to be interested in justice but that the judiciary could, and that justice must take precedence over any other interest. Jefferson, as president, felt that he had a more demanding responsibility, that of acting for the whole people, not just for one individual, and that he must himself determine what his duty required.

The circumstances were peculiar to the times—as the times were in 1807—and to the personalities involved. Aaron Burr had come to a period of his bizarre career when he felt capable of reaching abroad for the power he had failed to grasp at home. The sharing by himself and Jefferson of an equal vote for the presidency in 1800 had thrown the decision into the House of Representatives where Burr had lost. He had felt cheated and looked elsewhere for fulfillment of his ambitions. Jefferson regarded him as an adventurer, and they had long been avowed enemies.

Marshall's antagonism to Jefferson went back to the Federalists' defeat in the election of 1800 and the determination, noted earlier, of the Democratic-Republicans to reverse Federalist intentions. Marshall's attitude during Burr's trial in Richmond was expectable in one who saw himself as the sole defender of unionism in a regime otherwise devoted to dismantling the organization conceived by the Framers and established by Washington and Adams with notable assistance from

Hamilton. The Burr case came to trial three years after the *Marbury* decision and while Jefferson's frustration over Marshall's assertion of judicial supremacy was still acute. Jefferson might not control trials but he did control the apparatus of apprehension and prosecution, and when he became convinced that Burr was involved in a scheme to act with the British in a war against Mexico and in some fashion to establish an empire in the newly-acquired Louisiana Territory, he caused the arrest, and the transportation to Richmond for trial, of his old enemy.

Concerning the affair, Jefferson, in his annual message to the Congress, said that there had been an incipient "conspiracy" but that it had been circumvented. He named no names and the Congress asked for more information. To this he incautiously replied that his reference had been to Burr "whose guilt is placed beyond question." He said this on the authority of a letter from General Wilkinson, army commander on the southern frontier, who, however, seems to have been engaged in devious dealings with those who were maneuvering for advantage in the disturbed lower Mississippi country. He had evidently concluded that there was more to be gained by betraying Burr than going on with what now looked very like a risky adventure.

The charge against Burr was indeed treason and Jefferson was confident that he could be proven guilty. The Richmond prosecutor, John Hay, was disconcerted when at the trial Burr demanded that since Jefferson had brought the charge he should be required to support it in person. Hay at once asked for advice, and Jefferson replied:

> Reserving the necessary right of the president to decide, independently of all other authority, what

papers coming to him as president, public interests
permit to be communicated, and to whom, I assure
you of my readiness, under that restriction, voluntarily, to furnish on all occasions, whatever the
purposes of justice may require.*

This presidential message was less yielding than at
first appeared. The awareness of his responsibilities and
what they implied was just under the surface. This
presidential determination was revealed when he was
pressed for more concessions. His critics were activated,
and one of them, Luther Martin, who was friendly to
Burr, said of Jefferson's position that it had "the ring of
the untouchable sovereign" who was in reality "no more
than the servant of the people."

The issue was joined. There was a clash of implications. The Constitution did not give the president immunity from judicial process, but neither did it give the
courts power to invade another branch even in pursuit
of justice. In Marshall's view the necessity for this pursuit was to be decided by judges alone, and Jefferson's
assertion that his position as the determiner of what the
public interest required, was inadmissible.

The preamble had mentioned the establishment of
justice as one of the reasons for a constitution. In
Marshall's view the judiciary was responsible for its
administration. But Article II had made the president
the representative of all the people and had charged him
to faithfully execute the laws. It was Jefferson's understanding that how he should discharge these responsibili-

---

*This account, and the quotations from Jefferson's papers
follow the narrative of A. J. Beveridge's *Life of John Marshall*
(Boston: Houghton, 1919), p. 435 and *passim* .

ties was his concern, not that of the judiciary, and, for that matter, not that of the Congress either.

The issue became sharper as the controversy proceeded. Martin cited other instances of presidential refusal to disclose secret papers. Hay at first conceded that the president could be subpoenaed as a witness but that the judge ought not to grant such a request unless justice demanded it. Marshall, holding that the requirements of justice were to be determined by the Court, issued the writ. He adduced two reasons: (1) all accused persons had the right to compel the attendance of witnesses. Neither the Constitution nor legislation provided for exceptions. (2) If the president could be excepted it could only be because his duties . . . "demand his whole time for national objects." But this contention was not admissible since, he said, "it is apparent that this demand is not unremitting." Then there followed a typical Marshallian postscript. If, he said, the president *is* so occupied at the time, then "it would be sworn on the return of the subpoena, and would rather constitute a reason for not obeying the process than a reason against its being issued."

Marshall was establishing a precedent, one consistent with the claim of judicial supremacy in *Marbury*. The president, when the Court said so, was to be merely a citizen like any other. He might defer his appearance because of the claims of office, but he could not refuse. As in *Marbury*, Marshall gave way about the immediate claim but held to the permanent principle, thus giving Jefferson, again, no reason for reasonable complaint. There was a further exchange with Hay who maintained that in the instant case the summons for attendance, the subpoena *duces tecum*, called only for the submission of papers. Not so, said Marshall, the call for the papers was in addition to the demand for appearance.

Jefferson did not take Marshall's contention lightly. He responded in a letter to Hay (June 17, 1807). He argued that by forwarding the papers in question he had "substantially fulfilled the object of the court." He went on to say that because of "paramount duties to the nation at large" he had no obligation to comply with the summons. He might

> ... receive a similar one to attend ... trials ... in the Mississippi territory ... St. Louis and other places on the western waters, or at any place other than the seat of government. To comply with such calls would leave the nation without an executive branch, whose agency, nevertheless, is understood to be so constantly necessary that it is the sole branch which the constitution requires to be always in function. It could not, then, mean that it should be withdrawn from its station by an coordinate authority.

Jefferson did not end there. Marshall's demand that he personally appear was rejected, but, to be conciliatory, he did grant that papers might be called for and personnel examined by deposition. Even then there were exceptions, and he stated them:

> With respect to papers, there is certainly a public and a private side to our offices. To the former belong grants of land, patents for inventions, and other papers patent in their nature. To the other belong mere executive proceedings. All nations have found it necessary that, for the advantageous conduct of their affairs, some of these proceedings, at least, should remain known to their executive

functionary only. He, of course, from the nature of the case, must be the sole judge of which of them the public interests will permit publication. The respect mutually due between the constituted authorities, in their official intercourse, as well as sincere dispositions to do for every one what is just, will always insure from the executive, in excercising the duty of discrimination confided to him, the same candour and integrity to which the nation has in like manner trusted in the disposal of its judiciary authorities.

Even this was not quite all. Marshall was a formidable opponent, and he was intent on establishing the principle that only the judiciary could determine the demands of justice. Jefferson again insisted that, as president, he had an "unremitting" duty to *whole* people. This, he said, precluded his being made a servant of "a single individual." Furthermore, since the judiciary had constantly asserted that "the leading principle of our constitution" was the independence of the branches, what became of that independence if the president were subject to the commands of the judiciary "and to imprisonment for disobedience if the several courts could bandy him from pillar to post, keep him constantly trudging from north to south and from east to west, and withdraw him entirely from his official duties?"

If this was a confrontation, as the statements of the chief justice and the president seemed to make it, there was a curiously blunted conclusion. Burr was acquitted of treason, but afterward was held for trial on a charge of misdemeanor. The prosecutor had not produced the letters demanded in the subpoena *duces tecum*. Burr again demanded that these be produced; if they were not, he said, the president ought to be held in contempt. Jefferson was not quite so firm as he had been at first. He wrote to Hay:

> I hope . . . that the discretion of the C.J. will suffer this question to lie over for the present, and at the ensuing session of the legislature he have means provided for giving individuals the benefit of the testimony of the exec. functionaries in proper cases, without breaking up the government.

To this day no one knows what Jefferson had in mind, but it may well have been an amendment to the Constitution that would define presidential privilege. This, however, is speculation. Marshall seems never to have responded, or, perhaps Hay never passed on to him Jefferson's message. According to Beveridge there was a second subpoena *duces tecum* and to this Jefferson responded again in a letter to Hay simply refusing to sanction a proceeding so preposterous by "taking any notice of it."

So a president was for the first time required by a judge to submit to his demands. He did not; he maintained his presidential independence. Marshall also maintained his right to require submission to his decree; it was a standoff.

Until 1952 (in the *Steel* cases) no president would ever allow his power to be defined by a judge or judges. In spite of a magnificent dissenting opinion by Chief Justice Vinson, a majority held that Truman had exceeded his powers in seizing certain production facilities. Truman, without comment, abjectly surrendered. When Nixon, in 1974, was directed by the Court to surrender evidence, he also gave in, thus confirming the powers Marshall had claimed. These breaches of the separation principle were so generally approved that the long approach of the judiciary to supremacy seemed to have reached an end. Nixon's difficulty was that he had an even worse case than Truman's to stand on. Doubtful conduct was involved.

The Court's advantage lay in popular distrust of the incumbent president. If judges had usually been cautious about requiring a compliance they after all could not compel, they still did not abandon their claim of the right to do so. When they exercised it, however, they made sure that the circumstances were favorable. Even when they were not, as Marshall must have concluded when he contemplated Jefferson's popularity, or as Taney found when he opposed Lincoln, the confrontation was avoided but the principle was not abandoned.

In spite of the Court's impressive precedents, supremacy remained merely a claim, supported by implication, even after Nixon's surrender. The Constitution had not been amended; it had only been interpreted. When judges looked at the Constitution it must have given them some concern that only the president had a prescribed oath (or affirmation). It required him to "preserve, protect, and defend the constitution of the United States." It did not say that he should do this as prescribed by the Court; and the Court had no equivalent stated duty.

14: Congressional Privilege

During the first administration—Washington's—two constitutional precedents were sought to be established by the Congress. Both had to do with the expansion of its specified directives. It might be said that one attempt was lost and one was won, although it always has to be noted that such victories are conditional and not necessarily permanent.

The first of these attempts caused a controversy at once when a bill authorizing a department of foreign affairs was being considered. The Constitution did not say that the organization of departments was a legislative prerogative, but it did say that no money could be drawn from the Treasury but in consequence of appropriations made by law, and money could not be appropriated without saying to what agency it was to go. It seemed reasonable enough to conclude that the power to appropriate implied the power to designate its object. There was, however, the difficulty that the president had been given the duty of faithfully executing the laws and that he could hardly do this if he could not specify the means he would use and the assistance he would need. Washington did not insist on the prerogative. He allowed the Congress to say that the agency should be created, what its duties should be and what funds it should have. The veto he might have imposed was withheld. The Court was not asked to interpret the Constitution's words, and the precedent was established.

The second question had to do with the officials appointed to administer the departments. The directive was that unless otherwise provided they should be appointed by the president—but with the "advice and consent" of the Senate. Did this mean that the Senate should also approve dismissals? About this there unexpectedly arose a full-scale debate. Its settlement has sometimes been referred to as "the compromise of 1789." If the phrase is taken to mean that Washington and congressional leaders actually bargained and made some sort of deal there is no evidence that any such face-to-face trade-off occurred. Nevertheless there did emerge an arrangement with that effect. Executive departments were authorized by the Congress and would be in the future, but the president emerged with the power to appoint his subordinates, subject to confirmation by the Senate, and with power to dismiss them without interference.

That there was no argument about authorization was perhaps because the new government inherited a department of foreign affairs from the old Continental Congress as well as others for treasury and war. They did not have to be created; it was only necessary that funds should be provided. If the general duty to lay and collect taxes was taken to imply also the duty to designate what governmental agencies should be created to administer the appropriations, something the Constitution did not say, this was a vast widening by implication of a constitutional clause, the first in American history.

Unlike the question concerning governmental organization, the associated one about the dismissal of appointees caused serious controversy. There was among

Democratic-Republicans, a lingering hold-over of suspicion about executives. They tended to regard the
president as the successor of the British governors they
had so recently got rid of, and they were moved to resist
any expansion of his powers and even to limit or even
seize them if they could. It was because of this that they
insisted on approval of his dismissals as well as his
appointments.

Debate was heated. Madison, now a representative,
was active as usual in all that was going on. Curiously, in
spite of his affiliation with Jefferson, he made the case
for presidential control of subordinates. He saw no
alternative. He said so with characteristics lucidity:

> It is one of the most prominent features of the
> constitution, a principle that pervades the whole
> system, that there should be the highest possible
> degree of responsibility in all the executive officers
> thereof; anything, therefore, which tends to lessen
> this responsibility, is contrary to its spirit and
> intention, and unless it is saddled upon us ex-
> pressly by the letter of that work, I shall oppose
> the admission of it into any act of the legislature.

Madison's statement was immediately challenged by
William Smith of South Carolina, Theodore Bland of
Virginia, and James Jackson of Georgia. Jackson even
argued that heads of departments had independent constitutional status. John Page of Virginia spoke for this
group in opposing consent to any strengthening of the
executive; he referred directly to that "energy" in government, so often praised in *The Federalist*. It was, he
said:

> ... the true doctrine of tyrants ... [and] may be
> the destruction of liberty; it should not, therefore,

be too much cherished in a free country. A spirit of independence should be cultivated. . . . The liberty and security of our fellow-citizens is our great object, and not the prompt execution of the laws. Indecision, delay, blunders, nay villanous actions in the administration of government, are trifles compared to legalizing the full exertion of a tyrannical despotism. . . .

In reply, Madison spoke specifically about the president's powers of dismissal:

Vest this power in the senate jointly with the president, and you abolish at once the great principle of unity and responsibility in the executive department, which was intended for the security of liberty and the public good. If the president should possess alone the power of removal from office, those who are employed in the execution of the law will be in their proper situation, and the chain of dependence be preserved; the lowest officers, the middle grade, and the highest, will depend, as they ought, on the president and the president on the community.

It was the Federalists who supported Madison, especially Fisher Ames and John Laurence, but Elias Boudinot of New Jersey exposed most strikingly the absurdity of the proposal:

Who, then, are the parties? The supreme executive officer against his assistant; and the senate are to sit as judges to determine whether sufficient cause for removal exists. . . . But suppose they shall decide in favor of the officer, what a situation is the president then in, surrounded by officers with whom, by his situation, he is compelled to act, but in whom he can have no confidence.

This view prevailed. After days of debate a test vote (30 to 18) confirmed the president's power to remove the head of the department just being organized without the consent of the Senate.

This early conflict, and the way it was settled, was significant for another reason than that it recognized the president's executive authority. It might have been expected that the Constitution would be amended to provide the solution. In fact, the debate reads now, as so many have since, as though constitutional questions were being settled by the Congress. But legislatures cannot do this. Unless directives become part of the Constitution by amendment they are sure to be questioned sooner or later and usually at most embarrassing times. This one was, in 1867, when the tenure of office act was passed. That act, it will be recalled, forbade President Johnson to dismiss the secretary of war, E. M. Stanton. When he persisted, impeachment proceedings very nearly succeeded in driving him from office. There was, in fact, another attempt by the Senate in 1926 to prevent dismissal of a postmaster by the president.

The lesson in this is that constitutional questions require constitutional solutions, but Madison would have known this at the time of the Convention; why did he not insist on a method of amendment that would have made reliance on significant implications unnecessary?

When it came to the issue of presidential power in the first Congress, why was Washington satisfied with something less than amendment? It may have been—it can only be guessed—that he recognized the procedure as too formidable. He may well have doubted his ability to carry both houses by two-thirds, and may have had even stronger doubts about carrying three-quarters of the state legislatures. Populist sentiment was very strong and suspicion of executive power was only modified by his own prestige. Doubts were expressed repeatedly in the legislative debates, not always in such acidulous language as was used by Representative Page, but such as left no doubt of the Democratic-Republicans' belief that legislatures were the only true representatives of the people. They clearly felt that the separation principle ought not to be taken to be a limitation on the will of the Congress.

This was a difference that would persist throughout the following years. It would issue, for instance, in the agrarian movement of the late nineteenth century and would be the issue between Democrats and Republicans in several campaigns for the presidency.

The other important issue concerning congressional privilege, arose a few years later, after the ignominious defeat of General St. Clair who had been in command of an expedition to secure the western frontiers against repeated Indian raids. In March of 1792, the anti-Federalist Wm. B. Giles, introduced a House resolution requesting the president to investigate "the causes of the late defeat of the army under command of Major General St. Clair." John Vining inquired how it was proposed to proceed. Giles was evasive, so Vining suggested that the House require the officials "to give an account of their conduct."*

To this suggestion Wm. Smith demurred. This, he

---

*The references in this section are from The Annals of the 2nd Congress, March, 1792. These issues were discussed by Leonard D. White in *The Federalists: A Study in Administrative History* (New York: Macmillan, 1948); and by Stephen Horn in *The Cabinet and Congress* (New York: Columbia University Press, 1960), especially in "The Heritage of the Federalists."

noted, was the first time the House had proposed to look into the conduct of officers responsible to the president. Such an investigation would violate the principle of separated powers. The president would, of course, make his own inquiry, and the House ought not to intervene. Smith, being a Federalist, was joined by others. Hugh Williamson agreed that the resolution was of "doubtful propriety" and recommended that a select committee be appointed to report at a later date. This suggestion was approved and a committee of seven, with Thomas Fitzsimmons as chairman, began a study of the St. Clair defeat. This committee decided it must have information and asked for it from Secretary Knox of the War Department. They asked, indeed, for the original instructions concerning the disastrous expedition.

It was in this way that the implied power of the Congress to investigate the executive was asserted. The committee had exceeded its terms of reference and had gone on to demand documents, not from the president but from the secretary. Washington was disconcerted. He called a meeting of the cabinet to discuss the propriety of yielding to such a demand. He outlined various alternatives. The three secretaries and the attorney general asked for time to consider a response. When he met with them again, all agreed that the House might inquire and might ask for papers, but that the president should forward only those documents he believed would not jeopardize the public interest.

Thus were established two precedents destined to be the cause of repeated acrimonies in years to come. No one insisted that the issues were constitutional and that both the congressional power to investigate and the president's power to dismiss ought to be determined in a formal way. It was simply assumed that an agreement satisfactory to both president and the legislators would be sufficient.

What satisfied Washington would not please most of his successors, and what satisfied one select committee in 1791 would seem quite insufficient to later investigators. The officials in the St. Clair instance furnished copies of the requested papers and also offered to allow a clerk of the committee to verify their authenticity. This can only be described as a surrender.

Jefferson was one of those who advised Washington to furnish documents; whether he made any distinction between their submission by the president or by the secretary of war is not known. When, later on, he himself had to deal with an embarrassing demand for information it did not come from the Congress but from the judiciary in the person of Marshall; there was thus no question of distinction between the president and his officials. Still, in both instances the president's position was that information would be furnished only if he decided that the public interest required the submission. If he chose to withhold any part of it neither of the other branches could compel him to do so. He stood on the principle of executive independence—that is, the separation of powers.

It will be seen that all those involved were acting on implications. The president assumed that faithful execution of the laws was a locution only he could interpret. The Congress assumed that the right of inquiry was implicit in the power to legislate. The brevity of the Constitution's clauses was immediately revealed as a doubtful virtue, but there were no amendments; they remained too difficult.

In these extraconstitutional arrangements, worked out during the first administration, the legislature appears to have gained the most. The consignment to the Congress of the power to investigate was a matter of immense importance, and only less important was the power to determine the organization of the whole executive establishment.

Both issues involved an inevitable conflict among implications. If the Congress had to provide funds it might reasonably say what they were provided for. If the president must faithfully execute laws he could hardly do it unless he could designate the necessary agencies. To have given up the power to organize but to have kept the power to dismiss the officials he appointed, was a poor bargain—if it *was* a bargain. Then for the legislature not only to authorize the agencies of administration but to look into their subsequent behavior was an enormous assumption of authority. It may have been reasonable, but if so why was the Constitution not amended to make it legitimate? Clearly the proliferation of implications originated in the impractical provisions for amendment made by the Framers.

15: Appropriation and Spending

Other issues closely related to those of administrative controls are those having to do with appropriation and spending. These have become more significant with the passage of time and the growing size, complexity, and cost of government. Their most acute phases have appeared in more recent history and these cannot be said to have been early departures from the Constitution's intentions. Indeed, they cannot be said to be departures at all. They simply were not anticipated by the Framers and so can be called constitutional only in the sense that all serious issues concerning the distribution of powers and the responsibilities of officials must be covered in some way by the higher law. They ought not to be the object of interested bargaining. They will be spoken of only briefly.*

To be successful a government with separated branches needs above all to have anticipated their points of contact and the areas of joint action. That the Framers were aware of this and yet left the Constitution without definite assignments is one of the deficiencies needing correction or amplification. A serious conse-

*For extended explanation the reader is referred to Louis Fisher, *Presidential Spending Powers* (Princeton: Princeton University Press, 1975).

quence of brevity has been that each branch has arrived
at its allocation of power in contests with the others,
sometimes fierce ones. This process of adjustment is
pictured by its apologists as having been expected to
show in time what the relations ought to be; at this
point the assumption was, the Constitution would be
suitably modified to establish workable relations. As has
been suggested earlier, the latter part of this process has
never taken place. The difficulty of making amendments
has left relations in a state of suspension. It is not clear
how far the Court may go in defining the powers of
president or Congress. It is not clear that the Congress
may exercise oversight, or how much. It is not clear
what the president may do in emergency even when the
powers he uses have been conferred by acts of the
Congress. It is not clear whether the Congress, in appropriating funds may go beyond anticipated revenues or
how far beyond. It is not clear, in spending these funds,
to what extent administering agencies must be guided
by congressional directives.

This list of ambiguities could be considerably longer.
As they have appeared, and as their significance has
become more apparent, not one has resulted in clarifying amendment.

It may of course be that as in other matters, the
Framers simply did not anticipate the seriousness of
such struggles as that between president and Congress
over appropriations and their use or disuse. However
that may be, it is certain that they were not prescient
about the difficulty they imposed on the amending
process that might have defined the respective powers
after experience.

Lacking clarifying amendments, each branch has continued to possess with any security only such powers as

were conferred in the original. Each, however, has acquired a tenuous position in the scheme by an extension of what its successive occupants have regarded as reasonable implications. Certain of these are accepted by all, but these are few; most have been actively disputed. It is important to recall that when the Court assumes to define the powers of the other branches, it thereby defines its own.

The legislature assumes that it may arrange the organization of the executive and monitor its operations. The president assumes that the heads of all departments are his subordinates and that they may have only such relations with the Congress as he may allow. We have seen that these assumptions cannot be traced to any provision of the Constitution. They exist by implication, and, as we have also seen, a reasonable implication in the view of one may not be reasonable in the view of others. Attitudes are apt to change with time and circumstances, making any reference to constitutional meanings uncertain.

When, at about the middle of the second century of the government's operation, a dispute arose about what was called "impoundment," it called attention to the lack of directives for the appropriation and disposal of funds. The dispute was not new except in popular notice. It was one of those made inevitable by vagueness; moreover, it was only one phase of the wider area of government finance. This particular question was whether the president was obligated to spend or dispose of *all* the funds appropriated by the Congress and for the particular purposes nominated in the legislation.

There had been no difficulty about this so long as divergencies were not weighted by differences of policy. It was inevitable from the first that government operations could not be exactly measured to moneys provided in advance. There might be too much or too little. Too much would require a return of the surplus to the treasury; too little would make necessary a deficiency appropriation. Both these had usually gone on in routine fashion without raising hackles in any important way.

When, however, real disputes about policy appeared—when the Congress made appropriations for something the president felt strongly was mistaken and he refused to disburse the funds, there arose a furor about the Framers' intentions. It was in a way typical. Neither side of the dispute could point for justification to anything the Constitution actually said.

To approach the question of appropriations and the use by the executive of the appropriated funds, it is necessary to recall how deeply legislative supremacy is imbedded in American tradition and how deeply legislative hostility to the executive is similarly imbedded. For the Framers these traditions constituted one of their worst problems. As they sat in Philadelphia the failure of the Continental Congress was on everyone's mind. It had amply displayed administrative behavior that was slack and ineffective. It had attempted to manage the nation's affairs at first through committees and, when that arrangement proved impossible, through department heads elected by itself. A constitutional convention had been made necessary by the lack of an executive with independent powers who could act in the general interest. Still the Framers saw that he could not be anything like a king. After all, monarchical rule had just been repudiated. They decided that he would have to be chosen by a national electorate and would have to conduct his office in ways defined by a written undertaking approved by the people. Decidedly, the definition must not come from the legislature; nor must the legislature be allowed any part in administrative processes.

The Constitution, as written in Philadelphia and ratified by conventions in the states (whose delegates were elected by the people) did indeed recognize both the need for a separately chosen executive and the continuing belief that legislators, in spite of the president's popular election, were the representatives of their constituents and, when acting together, of the whole people. Both the president and the Congress were given a part in legislation, and this included the all-important matter of taxing and appropriating. Only the House of Representatives could originate taxes, although the Senate could "propose or concur with amendments," but as to appropriations, no money could be "drawn from the treasury, but in consequence of appropriations made by law." And laws required the signature of the president (although his veto could be overridden).

These provisions seemed to give the Congress the duty of making what was later called a budget—that is, a total of appropriations. In the earliest days it deliberated and came to conclusions about what was needed with minimum attention to what the president might think was required. Members had favorite projects, often ones of some use to their districts, and they traded votes with others who had other interests. This, as we know, developed into an annual compendium nicknamed the pork barrel. It proved to be a hardy survivor among legislative traditions. One of its characteristics was that in its making the budget concept was ignored. No one cared about the total.

The difficulty with this, apart from its irresponsibil-

ity, was that there were national interests apart from
and beyond those of any district and there was no one
in the Congress whose purposes—pleasing his constituents and getting reelected—including watching out for
them. Only the president, being elected by all the people, had responsibility for national interests. It was this
difference in constituency that caused the perennial
disputes between the branches concerning expenditures.

For years appropriations continued to be made without serious attention to the totals arrived at. Since
favorite projects of influential congressmen were funded
regardless of the government's income, these in time
became so excessive and so miscellaneous that the expectable criticisms arose. The indicated reform was the
gathering of spending proposals into a genuine budget,
put together by the president and submitted to the
congress for approval. It required an extended period of
agitation by outsiders for this proposal to make an
impression on a reluctant Congress, but it finally prevailed. In 1921 such a budgeting procedure was instituted but it was far from faithfully respected by legislators. They simply refused to give up their habit of
independent appropriation.

Only when the chronic disparity between income and
outgo resulted in an enormous and growing burden of
debt was some attempt made to establish a total within
which congressional spending would be confined. Such
an effort was made in 1946 and failed because its
limitations were ignored. No other attempt was made
until in 1974 the Congress went about to set up its own
budget. It is necessary to repeat what has been said
many times in this essay—this insistent competition with
the president is owed to constitutional ambivalence. The
two budget bureaus again represent the same claims to
one power that showed themselves in the earliest admin-

istrations. They do not represent departures from the Constitution so much as attempts to force the Constitution into patterns that exist only by implication. Such resorts may express the hostility and distrust of the branches for each other, but they make administration far more awkward and costly than it need be. Besides they do not settle the issue. Only amendment could do that.

It has been noted that differences about appropriating and spending were not really serious when government was small and the amounts involved were comprehensible. Even then, however, the principle involved was the subject of controversy between Federalists and Democratic-Republicans and showed that quarreling officials would only reach uneasy agreements.

In the first Congress a question arose concerning the specificity of appropriation. The Federalists wanted lump sums to be disposed of as administrators thought necessary; the Democratic-Republicans wanted the legislature to retain control in detail. Louis Fisher, exploring this matter* discovered, as he thought, that the difference was more in party rhetoric than in administrative reality. Actually, he concluded, executive discretion in spending has been a fact of life since the first administration. But the Congress has never been reconciled to the necessity. All through our history there have been echoes of the exchange Fisher reports between the proponents of executive freedom and congressional restraint in Washington's time:

> In 1793 representative Giles offered a number of resolutions charging Hamilton with improper use of national funds. The first resolution stated that

*In his *President and Congress* (New York: Free Press, 1972), pp. 116 ff.

"laws making specific appropriation of money should be strictly observed by the administrator of the finances thereof." Representative Smith of South Carolina proceeded to refute Giles point by point, arguing that the administration ought to be free to depart from congressional appropriations whenever the public safety or credit would thereby be improved. When exercised for the public good, executive spending discretion would "always meet with the approbation of the national legislature." All the Giles resolutions were subsequently voted down by the house.

This appears to be a typical collision between the legislative and executive branches, but the dispute was not so much constitutional as it was partisan and personal. It was Hamilton's colleague in the cabinet, Thomas Jefferson, who had drafted the resolutions for Giles. The author of Smith's effective rebuttal: Why, none other than Hamilton himself.

In spite of Fisher's comment on this early exchange it must be concluded that there was indeed a constitutional issue at stake. Directions governing the appropriating of money and its expenditure had not been provided, and, lacking them, executives and legislatures were embarked on two centuries of perennial quarreling.

No one knew, after many unhappy passages between the branches, where the spending power belonged. Could the Congress exercise control when the executive actually made the expenditures? If the Framers meant it that way they should have specified the means for controlling, and if the Congress still contended that its powers were so extensive, they might have been legitimated by amendment. They never have been.

16: Impeachment
(Blount, Pickering, and Chase, 1803–4)

Impeachment has been mentioned. This is another instance of ambiguity. The words used in the Constitution have been the subject of differences on several occasions of the utmost seriousness for the nation. The worst of these have been when presidents were involved. There have been, however, more cases involving "other officials," especially judges, and these, occurring in early years, first tested the designated procedures.

William Blount was a senator and his case has only the interest that it eliminated legislators from among the "civil officers" mentioned in the Constitution. This was a conclusion reached by the Senate, without discernible logic, or constitutional reference. John Pickering was a district judge who became an alcoholic and behaved reprehensibly on the bench. He was "removed," something not provided for either. But Samuel Chase was a Supreme Court justice. His trial was the first real test of the procedure. He had used his position to further Federalism at a time when Jefferson and the Democratic-Republicans were coming into control not only of the presidency, but of the Congress. His behavior was admittedly unbecoming, but whether it constituted impeachability was in question. He was tried but not convicted.

It was in these cases that a permanent legislative

stance showed itself. Since the House of Representatives was charged with bringing impeachments and the Senate with conducting trials, the whole process went on within the legislative branch. It will be recalled also that amendment was consigned wholly to legislators. It is not strange therefore that a process giving legislators the power of removal from office should not be amended to open the process to others, or even to a clarification of their doubtful competence. Monopolies are seldom given up voluntarily.

How captious and vindictive partisans could become was at once evident in the trials of Pickering and Chase. The prosecutors' arguments might be demolished and senators might even be convinced by the defense, refusing in the end to convict, but this had no effect on the legislators' claims. These claims were that they were empowered to impeach and convict for any reason they chose to find repugnant. The consistent view of defendants was, of course, that the House was acting improperly when it departed from what they contended were proper reasons, and these had to be indictable crimes, not merely behavior offensive to the prosecution.

The locution used in the Constitution is this (in Article II, Section 4):

> The president, vice president and all civil officers of the United States, shall be removed from office on impeachment for, and conviction of, treason, bribery, or other high crimes and misdemeanors.

This clause was adopted by the Convention after the terms "malpractice and neglect of duty" had been eliminated during preliminary discussions, thus seemingly discarding these as impeachable offenses, but behavior simply disapproved by the legislators was not to be a cause for impeachment; there must have been illegality. This formulation was not reached until, after a month of consideration and frustration in the attempt to make a more precise definition, a committee on detail, appointed to clarify several issues, was asked to report on this among others.

On August 6th the report was submitted. In it the earlier language was changed to "treason, bribery, and other high crimes or misdemeanors." And this was to remain permanent. The committee doubtless meant to clarify, and for this reason used terms they believed were precise, but as subsequent events showed they were not successful.

It was a prestigious committee: Rutledge, Randolph, Gorham, Ellsworth, and Wilson. Three of these were afterward justices of the Supreme Court and one was Washington's attorney general. Such membership makes it seem certain that the change of language adopted by them was meant to be understood as having legal connotations. What did those terms mean? There is no difficulty about treason or bribery. There would seem to be none either about high crimes. A high crime is obviously at a level above the ordinary. That would not be an offense against persons or property; it would be an official one, such, for instance, as violation of the oath of office or gross misuse of the power confided to an official. It might not be justiciable in any court but that provided for impeachments, but the charge would have to be suitably connected with duties and would have to be a violation of the Constitution.

Misdemeanor offers more difficulty and not only about the word itself but about its juxtaposition with "high crimes." Did the adjective "high" modify misdemeanors as well as crimes? There would be quarrels

about this arising from the legislative desire to keep
options open; that is, to make officials in other branches
subject to their judgment about conduct. These quarrels, indeed, would center in this legislative determination to maintain its supremacy in the governmental
system.

The committee on detail can hardly have meant to
make officials impeachable for common misdemeanors.
These, in legal language, are any crime less serious than
felony, putting them in a category that, in connection
with civil officials, would seem too trivial to have been
so prominently mentioned. The word "high" then must
have been meant to modify misdemeanor as well as
crime. There is also the crucial position in the wording
of "other." This could only mean that misdemeanors
were, like bribery and treason, in a category above the
ordinary. Impeachment was not to be for just any
departure from becoming conduct, it was to be for
conduct whose nature was measured by the preceding
treason and bribery, the worst of all indecencies for a
public official.

Dictionaries define the words misconduct and misdemeanor as synonyms, but legally, misdemeanor has an
entirely different meaning from misconduct. It is punishable behavior, and a high misdemeanor would be, like
high crime, an unusual offense. Taken together, and
applied to national officials, they can hardly be supposed to mean anything less serious than violation of
the official's oath. For the president this oath is specified:

> I do solemnly swear (or affirm) that I will faith-
> fully execute the office of president of the United
> States and will, to the best of my ability, preserve,
> protect, and defend the constitution of the United
> States.

For other offices there is no such specification, but of judges it is said that they shall hold their offices during "good behavior." This probably was again an attempt by the committee to be more precise. It was another traditional term. It meant permanent, *unless convicted in a process of impeachment.* It was alternative language for "incumbency for life." But legislators would uniformly interpret it as the simple opposite of ill behavior, and, in their view, ill behavior must be a cause for removal from office. For this, impeachment is the stated process, in fact, the only process. Here there appears another curiosity of the Constitution. There are directives for nomination and appointment; there are none for removal short of trial and conviction in the impeachment process.

Besides the general clause quoted above, several others in the Constitution mention impeachment. The first (in Article I, Section 2), assigns the power to the legislative houses:

> The house of representatives shall . . . have the sole power of impeachment.

The second (in Article I, Section 3) describes the trial:

> The senate shall have the sole power to try all impeachments. When sitting for that purpose, they shall be on oath or affirmation. When the president of the United States is tried, the chief justice shall preside; and no person shall be convicted without the concurrence of two-thirds of the members present.

This article also goes on to a qualification:

> Judgment in cases of impeachment shall not extend further than to removal from office, and disqualification to hold and enjoy any office of

honor, trust, or profit under the United States, but the party convicted shall nevertheless be liable and subject to indictment, trial, judgment, and punishment according to law.

Still another reference occurs later on (in Article III, Section 2):

The trial of all crimes, except in cases of impeachment, shall be by jury.

This certainly seemed to say that crimes by officials were impeachable, but did it mean that *only* crimes were impeachable? This interpretation legislative prosecutors would never admit, and defenders of those on trial would always claim. Both could and did appeal to the Constitution's language for support. Misdemeanors, trials, and convictions, like high crimes, are words with criminal connotations. Relying on this, defenders always insist that indictable offenses must be charged. Prosecutors, in contrast, always insist that the House may define impeachable offenses in any way it prefers.

These were the ambiguous constitutional clauses governing the process entered on when Senator Blount, Judge Pickering and Justice Chase became the unfortunate defendants in early impeachment proceedings. There had as yet been no occasion for a taking of sides on the dividing issue; but in these earliest trials attitudes became firm. The choice between them would never be made in the only definitive way—by amendment. They would remain preferences to be made good in trials of strength.

William Blount was a senator from Tennessee. A House committee in 1797 moved that he be impeached. The first question was whether members of the Congress came within the category of "civil officials." But another soon arose. Before he could be tried he was expelled from the Senate; did this end his liability to impeachment? Could a private citizen be subjected to the process?

Blount was alleged to have plotted with the British, who were at war with Spain, to invade Florida. He had written a letter admitting that he would be "at the head of the matter on the part of the British." James Carey, an interpreter, to whom the letter was written, allowed President Adams to come into its possession. He, in turn, forwarded it to the House for such action as it should care to take. The inference was that in his view senators were impeachable. The House adopted the procedure that would be followed consistently afterward. A committee recommended charges; the House voted to accept them; it then appointed managers to present its case, and forwarded them to the Senate where the trial was to take place.

Representatives Bayard and Harper, House managers, at once put forward a precedent-setting argument. This was that "impeachment," like other terms in the Constitution such as "felony," "habeas corpus," "privileges and immunities" and "attainder," had been "drawn from their import in the books of common law." It was pointed out that the Constitution had not described the persons who should be the objects of impeachment, "nor defined the cases to which the remedy shall be confined." It must be presumed, then, that "we are designedly left to the regulations of the common law." If this was accepted, of course, the question was "What persons, for what offenses, are liable to be impeached by this rule?" The answer was that "all of the King's subjects are liable to be impeached by the Commons and tried by the Lords, upon charges of high crimes and misdemeanors."

As to William Blount, the articles submitted by the

House held that since the Constitution was merely silent as to who might be impeached (besides the president, vice president and civil officers), he might properly be tried. Also, as to the offenses for which persons might be impeached, since not a word was to be found in the Constitution, it was left to the House of Representatives, "to whom the power of impeachment in all its latitude, and with all its properties and incidents, is given."

There is a concise and useful account of this debate in Irving Brant's study of the Constitution's meaning.* He points out that it occurred at a time of acrimony between Federalists and Democratic-Republicans caused by the French revolution. John Adams's alien and sedition laws had outraged Jefferson and his followers. James A. Bayard, of the House managers, linked the Blount trial with the current Federalist fears of insurrection by using the illustration of a federal judge who, "forgetting his duty . . . instead of using his authority . . . to quell the insurgents, should aid them in their violence. Surely this would not be an official act; and shall I be told, for that reason, that he shall not be liable to impeachment? How else is he to be removed?"

This, of course, was a claim of general legislative power to impeach. Bayard's position would allow a partisan House to initiate and carry through the trial of any citizen who disagreed with its majority. This applied clearly, at that moment, to Jefferson, among others. He, as a candidate for the presidency in 1796, had been accused continually by Federalist editors of conspiring with France against the United States. Combined with

*Irving Brant, *Impeachment: Trials and Errors* (New York: Knopf, 1972).

the alien and sedition acts, impeachment was to suppress the rising Democratic-Republican movement. Jefferson, for instance, might be removed from the vice-presidency and could not escape by resigning. He could, indeed, be made perpetually ineligible for another office.

Moreover, as Brant remarks, Jefferson's Kentucky resolutions and Madison's Virginia resolutions in 1798 were intended to subvert the sedition act, making their sponsors ready objects for impeachment if the legislature, for any cause it chose, could bring a charge and hold a trial. The Federalists regarded these resolutions as subversive incitements to disunion, not perhaps actually crimes but deserving condign punishment.

Why, in that time of extreme partisanship and exaggerated Federalist fear, did the House managers fail to have their case accepted? There was a strongly Federalist Senate, but there proved not to be two-thirds who were willing to say that impeachment was a universal liability. A vote on this issue was avoided because a head count disclosed a shortage. There was, however, a finding that neither senators nor private persons were impeachable. Aside from this, the Constitution's clauses were left undefined. The House had not retreated from its position. It had simply retreated from decision in one trial.

In the action against Judge John Pickering of New Hampshire in 1803, the threat of impeachment came from the Democratic-Republicans, but again from the legislative branch. Adams had been defeated and Jefferson was now president, but the judiciary remained in Federalist control as the result of Adams's appointment of sixteen new judges under the last-minute bill creating a circuit court system. Jefferson, however, caused the act to be repealed and refused to allow Madison to deliver the commission to several justices of the peace who had also been appointed under the old act. (It was this refusal that gave rise to the *Marbury* case).

Impeachment seemed to the Democratic-Republicans as ready a partisan weapon as it had recently seemed to the Federalists when they had had a majority. A convenient opportunity to embarrass the Federalists presented itself in the misbehavior of Pickering who had repeatedly been drunk on the bench and had used abusive and obscene language. There was no doubt about the facts. Pickering was a disgrace to the judiciary. The question was whether such conduct constituted grounds for impeachment. Were his offenses high crimes or misdemeanors? The Senate, when it came to this issue, was unwilling to say that this was true. So it accepted the facts as presented by the House and declared itself of "the opinion that John Pickering be removed from the office of judge."

To remove without impeaching was obviously an abandonment of constitutional justification. It was, in effect, a claim that the legislature could remove for any cause it chose. It could merely disapprove the behavior exhibited by the accused and vote his removal. It had indeed done just that.

Since Samuel Chase was a member of the Supreme Court his case was more important. He happened also to be the object of special dislike by the Jeffersonians because of his activism in the Federalist cause, and not only in his private capacity. He had thundered Federalist convictions from the bench. His removal seemed a convenient way to remake the Court. Naturally, however, this motive, even if freely talked about, was not put forward as the cause for his impeachment. The charges carefully cited the Constitution's language, assuming a particular view of its meaning. The trial opened all the issues raised by conflicting interpretations. Were only indictable crimes impeachable? Or were offenses, not indictable, sufficient—such, for instance, as conduct not approved by his critics? If so, was the citation of that conduct by the House, and acceptance of it by the Senate, a proper cause for impeachment?

The first three charges laid against the justice by the House related to a case of one John Fries who had been tried by Chase for treason, found guilty and sentenced to death. Fries had organized a Pennsylvania Dutch resistance to certain taxes. The case was six years in the past and Fries had been pardoned by Adams, who had found the Chase conviction too much even for his intolerant nature. The House articles said that in the trial Chase had prejudiced the minds of the jury and unduly restricted defense counsel, "thereby preventing claims that the constitution had been misconducted."

The next five articles concerned another trial, that of one Callender, indicted under the sedition act, whose offense had consisted in writing, during the campaign of 1800, "Take your choice, then, between Adams, war, and beggary, and Jefferson, peace, and competency." The trial had been conducted, it was charged, with "manifest injustice, partiality, and intemperance."

There were similar allegations of prejudice in the conduct of other trials. Among these was a charge that the justice had delivered to a Maryland grand jury "a political harangue with intent to excite the fears and resentment of the said grand jury, and of the good

people of Maryland, against their state government and
constitution and ... against the government of the
United States."

Pressing the sufficiency of these allegations were
House managers John Randolph of Virginia (chairman),
George W. Campbell of Tennessee (later senator and
secretary of the treasury), Caesar Rodney of Delaware
(later Jefferson's attorney general), Joseph H. Nicholson
of Virginia (later a federal judge), and Peter Early of
Georgia. The defense had equally distinguished counsel.
It included Robert Goodloe Harper (himself a member
of the House), Luther Martin (attorney general of Maryland), Joseph Hopkinson of Philadelphia, and Charles
Lee, Washington's last attorney general.

The central issue concerning impeachment was here
being argued. What was the meaning of the few words in
the Constitution? Were they inclusive or merely indica-
tive? Could the legislators interpret them to mean that
merely repugnant conduct would be sufficient or must
it be proven that it was clearly criminal in the legal
sense? The trial chamber reverberated with impassioned
oratory, especially that of the eccentric and egotistical
John Randolph. Others were hardly less voluble. Manager Early contended that Chase had "violated the
sacred charter of our liberties" and had stained "the
pure ermines of justice by the political party spirit."
Manager Campbell tried to escape the literal and legalis-
tic confines of "high crimes and misdemeanors" by
contending that removal from office could not be considered a punishment for crime; it was merely a depriva-
tion of rights. He went on to state what would be the
thesis of all subsequent legislative prosecutors:

> Impeachment, therefore, according to the constitu-
> tion, may fairly be considered a kind of inquest

into the conduct of an officer, merely as it regards his office; the manner in which he performs the duties thereof; and the effects his conduct therein may have on society. It is more in the nature of a civil investigation than of a criminal prosecution.

He went on:

Hence I conceive that in order to support these articles of impeachment, we are not bound to make out such a case as would be punishable by indictment in a court of law. It is sufficient to show that the accused has transgressed the line of his official duty, in violation of the laws of his country, and that this conduct can only be accounted for on the ground of impure and corrupt motives.*

He was answered by Hopkinson for the defense, whose position was at the opposite extreme. No judge, he contended, could be impeached but for an indictable offense. He went on to lay bare the weakness of the other interpretation:

The constitution, sir, never intended to lay the judiciary thus prostrate at the feet of the house of representatives, the slaves of their will, the victims of their caprice. . . .

He asked whether the House could

. . . create offenses at their will and pleasure, and declare that to be a crime in 1804 which was an indiscretion or pardonable error, or perhaps an approved proceeding in 1800? . . . If this be truly the case, if this power of impeachment may be thus extended without limit or control, then in-

---

*This and other quotations from the trial of Justice Chase were cited by Brant, *Impeachment*, ch. 4.

deed is every valuable liberty prostrated at the foot of this omniponent house of representatives. . . .

Luther Martin and Robert Goodloe Harper expanded the contention that the Framers had never intended impeachment to be at the whim of the legislative branch. Harper struck at the managers' contention that the process was merely "in the nature of an inquest of office." If a conviction and removal was not a punishment but "the mere withdrawal of a favor of office granted, I ask," he said, "why this formality of proceeding, this solemn apparatus of justice, this laborious investigation of facts?"

> Everything by which we are surrounded informs us that we are in a court of law. . . . we are not engaged in a mere inquiry into the fitness of an officer for the place he holds, but in the trial of a criminal case on legal principles.

So the managers for the House and the distinguished lawyers for the defense stood in plain and precise opposition. Either impeachment was restricted to indictable crimes or it was definable by the legislators and could be whatever they chose to consider offensive.

At about this point in the trial a complication was introduced. Manager Nicholson pointed out that judges hold their commissions "during good behavior":

> The plain and correct inference to be drawn from this language is that a judge is to hold his office so long as he demeans himself well in it; and whenever he shall not demean himself well, he shall be removed.

There was a long legal history behind this phrase and Nicholson, followed by Rodney, recounted it in some detail. What it came down to was that a judge who had "misbehaved"—by favoritism, dereliction of duty, or offensive conduct on the bench—had violated his oath of office. This was an indefinite extension of impeachable conduct. It was difficult to counter for two reasons. There *was* the locution in the Constitution. The opposite of good behavior *was* ill behavior. And there was no provision for removal except by impeachment.

There was also the difference between officials who were to serve during good behavior and those, such as the president, who were elected for a term, something taken no account of by the Framers. The president, also, was accountable to the voters; "other officials" were not.

When Randolph closed for the managers he called up his reserves of eloquence. He may have been loud and bizarre, but he hit on the solid contention that the oath of office constituted a law and its violation was without question impeachable. No construction of meanings, no extension of implication was needed. The oath taken by Chase had required him "to dispense justice faithfully and impartially and with respect to persons." He had not done so. He had "demeaned himself amiss— partially, unfaithfully, unjustly, corruptly." It was not convicing. No one doubted at the end that Chase had been unfair, biased, contentious, and oppressive; but he had not been corrupt or unfaithful. Even six of the Jeffersonian senators joined the Federalists in refusing to act on the charges.

These contenders could find no substantial support for their positions. It was true that Hamilton had discussed impeachment several times in *The Federalist,* most importantly in No. 64. But in that essay he was mostly approving the Senate as the place for trials. Where else, he asked, could there have been "a tribunal sufficiently dignified or sufficiently independent?" He went on at some length about this. Nowhere, however, did he define an impeachable offense. The paragraph in question began by asking what was "the true spirit of the institution.... Is it not designed as a method of national inquest into the conduct of public men?" If this was so, he asked, who could "so properly be the inquisitors for the nation, as the representatives of the nation themselves?"

If it was to be a "national inquest" there need be no definition at all. Confinement to indictable offenses was ruled out, and the way was open to legislative determination of behavior. A public official—except a legislator—who had offended a majority of the Congress was impeachable. There might be differences among the legislators about the enormity of transgressions, but it would be settled by voting, and voting required no explanation. Madison also, during a debate in the Convention about impeachment for "maladministration" had objected that this would be "equivalent to tenure during the pleasure of the senate." But this word had been eliminated; so Madison offered no assistance.

"High crimes and misdemeanors" was substituted by the Convention for "maladministration." Nevertheless, as Brant contends, maladministration did perfectly describe the concept "that had been inching up on us for nearly a hundred years.... Germinating in an almost invisible crack in the limitation against abuse of impeachment (that is, the small opening created by the absence of a definition of 'high crimes and misdemeanors'), this false growth threatens to split the rock of the constitution."*

What this view, so neatly summarized, comes down to

*Brant, ibid., 176.

is that "serious dereliction from public duty," amounting to violation of the oath of office, is the only tenable cause for impeachment. Was this what the Framers meant by "high crimes and misdemeanors?" This is an interpretation consistently rejected by legislators. It was, in fact, rejected in the early cases cited here, and, as we have seen, Hamilton, Madison's colleague in writing *The Federalist,* rejected it too. His "inquest of the nation" was as wide open an approach as could well have been devised.

Morris, at the Convention, did speak of the executive, as did also James Wilson, who, next to Morris, seems to have been most concerned that the presidency should be suitably protected. In one instance Morris expressed emphatic opposition to any provision for a president's impeachment since it would weaken him unacceptably. Besides, failure to be reelected was sufficient punishment for ill conduct. The voters, both Morris and Wilson thought, would in due time attend to presumptuous presidents. As the Constitution finally stood, the president's powers were limited. His check on the legislature was a conditional veto of its acts, but the legislature's check on him was the power of unconditional ouster.

There was not so much concern with the impeachment of judges, but the definition of actionable offenses was equally important and caused the same division between those who claimed a sweeping interpretation of the legislature's powers and those who believed this interpretation exposed the tenure of both presidents and judges to congressional caprice. There is a presumption, however, to be drawn from the Convention's proceedings that this interpretation is inconsistent with the theory of checks and balances. That principle would give each, as Madison put it, some control in the business of the others, but would give none an absolute control. In the early impeachments the House managers claimed unlimited latitude. If the Congress voted to exercise it, however, there was no way of reviewing the decision. Only an amendment could modify or remove the congressional power to discipline the officials of other branches.

It may be added, as a kind of footnote here, that the Framers can hardly have anticipated that proceedings of the sort they prescribed would grip the nation's attention, arouse legislators' appetites for publicity, and go on for months, monopolizing communications, and drowning other public business in floods of speech. Like much else this danger would be given new dimensions by the invention of television, an irresistible attraction to politicians. This prolonged country-wide disturbance would, in fact, prove intolerable. The accused would find himself forced to resign if opinion should consolidate against him. The actual impeachment and trial of a president would be unlikely ever to reach a conclusion.

The Framers could not have anticipated all this, but they need not have precluded procedural accommodation to inevitable change. There was, it must be remembered, no other means provided for involuntary removal. The case of President Nixon was illustrative, but anyone reading the comments afterward would have been thoroughly confused. It was widely insisted that what had happened showed how perceptively wise the Framers had been; that at least when a president was involved the constitutional process had "worked." The fact was that it had failed. The prescribed process, if allowed to run its course, might have caused national disaster.

17: Delegation

The excuse offered earlier for so brief a discussion of problems associated with appropriation and spending must be used also in the discussion here of delegation. Its extensive employment did not begin until nearly a century after the adoption of the Constitution and then because of entirely new developments in private enterprise. To have anticipated the country's condition in the 1880's from the situation in the 1780's would have required something more than foresight. The Framers would have had to be seers. It was when industrialism began to impose itself on rural America that controls became necessary. If the growth of business could not be stopped, it could at least be made to behave fairly to those it affected. In this, as in other matters seeming to require amendment, that method of meeting the issues was avoided in favor of finding, however improbably, that the Constitution as written could be interpreted to allow the doing of what needed to be done.

What needed to be done was to restrain and regulate businesses grown so powerful that they were strangling smaller competitors and exploiting consumers. More was needed also than recourse to the common law principle that enterprises holding themselves out to serve the public could be required to serve all alike and on reasonable terms. Such businesses were called public utilities and were subject to the police power of the states. But the federal government had no comparable police power; and businesses other than public utilities needed to be regulated. Interstate commerce had constitutional mention. And to the clause permitting its regulation could be added the powers of the "necessary and proper" clause. There was then no insuperable difficulty in finding ways to control the railways which were the first object of indignation, especially among farmers who were infuriated by excessive charges for hauling their produce to market.

It was when public outrage caused the demand for the regulation of monopolies other than those classified as public utilities that the Constitution had to be stretched to find justification. The way taken to control the railways was not only to hold them within the principles governing common callings but to establish a commission charged with continuously maintaining fair practices and moderate rates. The Interstate Commerce Commission would be the forerunner of such other regulatory agencies during the next half century as the Communications, Power, Federal Trade and Securities and Exchange Commissions. Besides, such departments as Agriculture, Interior, Labor, Commerce, and Health, Education and Welfare would be given the duty by legislation of regulating the use of the public domain, produce markets, public health, conditions of work and wages, the quality of consumer goods and much else.

In the course of developing this immense area of governmental activity, requiring vast numbers of employees, questions of constitutionality arose repeatedly. Those who sought to justify it could find a small beginning in an incident having to do with the Embargo Act of 1809 (in the case of the *Brig Aurora*; 7 Crouch 383);

but it was in 1825 that the first standard for legislative delegation was established in *Wayman* vs. *Southard* [10 Wheat 1]. In that case Justice Marshall distinguished "important subjects, which must be entirely regulated by the legislature itself, from those of less interest, in which a general provision may be made, and power given to those who are to act under such general provisions to fill up details."

This distinction was evasive. Any regulation of consequence has to do with more than "filling up the details" omitted in legislative acts. Nevertheless, it would be subsequently relied on in many instances when much more was being done than this phrase implied. It became one of those fictions that were taken to be fact whenever convenient, and spread itself over a larger and larger area.

The distinction was made possible by the Constitution's silence on the power of the legislature to delegate beyond the making of laws to effectuate the seventeen powers enumerated in Section 8 of Article I.

These did not include delegation nor could any of them be stretched to include it. Furthermore, there was the limit imposed by the well-known dictum of Locke whose authority was practically biblical for American lawyers:

> The power of the legislative being derived from the people by a positive and voluntary grant and institution, can be no other than what the positive grant conveyed, which being only to make laws, and not to make legislators, the legislative can have no power to transfer their authority of making laws and place it in other hands.

How is it that, faced with this clear prohibition, regulatory bodies should have been given or have taken the power to create the vast body of administrative law that was to govern so much private activity?

Adequate description of the evasions permitting this development is beyond the stated scope of this essay, but a brief answer to the question may be ventured. It has to do, as would be guessed, with the gradual enlargement of implication. The theory has been that if the legislature sets standards and gives direction to the regulatory agencies, it is not delegating the power to legislate, only to carry out the will of the Congress, a matter of convenience.

If it is first admitted that there must exist power to regulate in the public interest, it is easy enough to justify the sloughing off of regulatory duties by the legislature. It is not something the Congress is physically capable of doing.

A set of politicians elected for limited terms, having to consider legislation for widely ranging purposes, could not possibly form itself into a bureaucracy capable of disciplining large enterprises. This fact, together with the need for exerting controls in the public interest, made delegation to permanent agencies necessary and more necessary as private businesses grew in size and scope. The "filling up of details" by these agencies, a fiction even in the early 1800's became patently unreal as the century wore on. For some delegations, such as giving administrative agencies the duty of making regulations, it was denied that these were legislative acts. The courts began to speak of the need in such instances for the Congress to supply standards. These, however, tended to become broader and more general. The Interstate Commerce Commission, for instance, was to fix rates that were "just and reasonable."

There was an extension of this in the so-called "contingency legislation." This granted the designated agency the authority to determine such facts as would bring laws into effect or, on occasion, suspend them. This was the issue in the *Brig Aurora* case, and it would arise in a series of later cases, the leading one being *Field* vs. *Clark* (143 U.S. 649) in 1892. In this case flexible arrangements included in the McKinley Tariff Act were in question. Of them the Court said that when the Congress "declared that when the suspension should take effect upon a named contingency 'there was no delegation of legislative powers, only the duty of finding fact.' "

There had been more than a century of such permissive opinions when, to everyone's surprise the Court in 1935 ruled (in *Panama Refining Co.* vs. *Ryan,* 293 U.S. 388) that the Congress had not met constitutional standards when it had given the president authority to exclude from interstate commerce oil produced in excess of state regulations. This "hot oil case" was the first of several rejections by the Court of Roosevelt's New Deal laws. Of these the most important was *Schechter Poultry Corp.* vs. *United States* (295 U.S. 495). This opinion declared that the Congress, in the N.R.A. act, had delegated legislative powers that were "unconfined and vagrant." Another opinion in the following year (*Carter* vs. *Carter Coal Co.,* 298 U.S. 238) invalidated an act because it delegated power to set up a code for regulating the coal industry. There was double objection to this—as there had been to the code-making provisions of N.R.A. It not only delegated legislative powers but delegated them to private bodies.

These latter rejections of delegation are usually spoken of as part of the conservative reaction to the New Deal. But even New Dealers were forced to admit that the delegation of such powers to code-making authorities went far beyond the limits set by the dictum of Locke. If it was necessary to delegate powers to make law the Constitution must say so.

There was a return to permissiveness after the early New Deal cases. The last objection to delegation was in 1939 when Justice Roberts said of the standards set up to govern the secretary of agriculture in the regulation of markets were "so vague as in effect to invest him with uncontrolled power of legislation." Roberts, however, did not prevail. A majority upheld the act. During the exigencies of World War II, both price and rent controls were approved. At one point Chief Justice Stone spoke of the Constitution as "a continually operative charter of government." It did not, he said, "demand the impossible or the impracticable." In spite of this modern tendency to ignore the Lockean rule it cannot be concluded that the Congress has unlimited power to delegate its law-making powers. As was shown by the resurgence of adverse opinions in the New Deal cases, there may at any time be a return to the stricter rule. Chief Justice Hughes did say that the Constitution was what the justices said it was, but he did not say which justices, nor did he say that justices might not reverse what former ones had said.

Considering the sudden decision of the Court to take a narrow view of congressional delegations of power in the New Deal cases—when the liberal Justice Cardozo spoke of one of them as "delegation run riot"—it seems quite possible that it might occur again. After another interlude of permissiveness some justice, recalling Locke and searching the constitution for any permissive hint, might find himself unable to agree that some regulatory body had properly constrained a plaintiff. Perhaps the regulating of some industry may have gone beyond congressional standards and amounted to legislation. The justice might convince his associates and a decision might result that would have the same devastating effect as the N.R.A. decision in 1935. That decision ended attempts at self-government for industry from which the Rooseveltians had hoped so much. The whole body of administrative law and indeed, regulation itself might be found in jeopardy.

A number of ingenious devices are used to evade the Lockean rule but most of them depend on varieties of oversight. They include concurrent resolutions, provisions for mandatory review, and periodical reporting to committees or even committee chairmen. The difficulty is, of course, that oversight itself is constitutionally suspect. To base the devices for evading the rule of nondelegation on oversight is to justify one implication by citing another. It is true that questions about the legitimacy of oversight have all but disappeared. It has indeed become the favorite cure among those who deplore the excesses of the executive branch. If experience is to be trusted, however, its devices are more likely to forward legislative intrusions than to become a reliable watchkeeping process. To adapt Justice Cardozo's locution, administrative law, when it exceeds the limits of legislatively directed regulation, is implication run riot.

The integrity of the Constitution is not safeguarded by contests among the branches even when they result in compromises satisfactory to the contestants.*

---

*For further consideration of the constitutional difficulty in justifying delegation, a study by Sotirios A. Barber may be consulted: *The Constitution and the Delegation of Congressional Power* (Chicago: University of Chicago Press, 1975).

18: Uncertain Procedures

By the end of the Jeffersonian succession (1825) amendment was no longer looked to for accommodation of the Constitution to circumstances. Implication had become the favored method. Brevity and generality allowed one or another branch to assume powers not clearly allocated to it, the most important expansion being judicial. The Court had gradually made itself the arbiter of limits for advance into unmarked territory, including its own. But brevity and generality also left vast areas to be occupied by interests outside as well as inside government. Consensus had been reached on almost none of the assumed permissions to act. On the contrary, most of them had engendered conflicting opinions and gathered powerful sources of support. They were still fluid, still the subject of proliferating litigation and wavering Court opinion.

Such issues as would arise in future governmental crises—domestic disputes, depressions, civil or foreign wars—would be determined by adversary action too. No excesses of any branch—and all would offend in this way—would be punishable or even reversible except by bargaining between the antagonists. The Constitution simply did not anticipate the settlement of such disputes. Worse, it did not provide a workable means for escaping from, relaxing, or adding to, constitutional directives. Only a reformed amendment procedure could do that.

In the Civil War Lincoln would behave in deliberately doubtful fashion just as Jefferson had, and would make the same explanation—that some provisions of the Constitution had to be ignored to save the rest of it. In later wars the imaginative term "emergency" would permit the concentration of powers in the presidency. It was the same recourse that provided freedom to meet the exigencies of the great depression of the 'thirties.'

Because the complexities of technology required controls beyond the capacity of the Congress, presidents assumed responsibilities—or had responsibilities thrust upon them—not even hinted at in the Constitution. We have seen these positions beginning to be assumed, and their justifications developing, in the first years after 1789 when the government began its operations.

In the succeeding contests presidents had a certain advantage. The Congress grew until it consisted of 535 members who were progressively less capable of using the powers they claimed. One reason for this was their concentration of time and effort on services for their local constituents. The attention they spared for national affairs became more and more marginal. This, together with the confusion inherent in numbers, made the branch hopelessly ineffective.

Confusion was compounded by sporadic ventures into oversight. Concerning this there would be a "compromise of 1921" to match in significance the "compromise of 1789." It has been noted that in the earlier arrangement the Congress gained the right to authorize governmental organizations and the president gained the right to dismiss—and therefore to control—his subordinates. In the later tradeoff (1921) the president gained an executive budget and the Congress a controller general. The budget would in time lead to inroads on appropriating powers by the executive. The controller general would regularize, and, to an extent, make effective, congressional interferences with executive operations. Like so many arrangements, both of these would exist in a kind of constitutional limbo. They were landmark concessions for both branches to have made, but it has to be said that they merely followed precedents established in the government's first presidential administration. The branches, in conflict, traded powers they did not possess and ignored the problem of legitimacy.

Similarly "emergency" with its categories of "limited" and "full," was no more than a refinement on Jefferson and Lincoln, the difference being that in the earlier instances there had been limits of time. Emergencies would still be in force several decades after Roosevelt when the nation was not at war—even an undeclared one—and not in the throes of depression.

The impeachments of the early years disclosed all the uncertainties encountered in later ones, even those of Presidents Andrew Johnson and Richard M. Nixon. Neither of these resulted in amendments calculated to clarify the process. Even the intention of the Framers was still the subject of controversy. Did they intend presidential impeachments to be part of their system of checks, or was it to be, as Hamilton described it, an inquest of the nation?

As we have seen, the differences about this would be as divisive in the 1970's as they had been in the early 1800's. They had surfaced in the 1860's and had been left unsettled. They were an illustration of the general agreement that amendment should not be resorted to in controversies about constitutionality. This left the situation exactly where it had been before the contest. The next impeachment would find the legislators resolved to act on their own assessment of offensive conduct. The defendants would protest that only genuine criminal offenses were impeachable.

The effects of this uncertainty have been described before and with sufficient variation, but causes have not been explored. It is not enough to say that the Framers made the original mistake of adopting an impractical procedure. There must be a deeper cause than this. The operative clause could after all have been amended at any time if there had been demand for it, but there was none.

The explanation must lie in a general willingness to overlook departures, however gross. This could only happen when there was the pretense that what was being done was not happening. Attenuations from time to time were said to be merely interpretations, a word, it may be repeated, not to be found in the Constitution. The doctrine of a "living Constitution" was indeed agreed to without making the life of the "living" document referable to any new principles of government or any new rules for mutual behavior. Strangest of all, for a professing democracy, the living—that is to say the altering—was consigned to a Court whose credibility as democratic was precisely nil. Its members were appointed for life. Besides, its judgments were reached after a slow and costly procedure, and its decrees were often arrived at by a close majority vote.

It is quite true that a government of interdependent powers must have a means of reaching conclusions when conflicts arise. It is quite true also that such a body might well be called a Court, but however named, it ought to have directives. It must watch for discrepancies between circumstances and the supreme law, and it must recommend to the people in some fashion the changes necessary to restore relevancy, but it ought to stop short of legislating. As we have seen, this was obvious to Jefferson. It was not obvious to Hamilton, or, under Hamilton's guidance, to Washington; these statesmen were Federalists and Federalists were not democrats. They believed in governance by "the rich and well born." The "people" they spoke of were the small number of white, male, property owners who made up the electorate of their time. They obviously thought the Court would always be safely conservative. We have seen how Hamilton's dictum that a government had inherent power to implement its assigned responsibilities opened the way to judicial supremacy; also how Marshall grasped it. It has never been surrendered.

It was in these ways, and for these reasons that constitutional adaptation came into the possession of an exclusive body established not for governmental but for private and adversary legal purposes. This is where the return of the Constitution to the people must begin. It is necessary, indeed, to go back to where this essay began and ask again: What is the difference between constitutional and other kinds of government?

It was a unique gift that the Framers presented to Americans for their approval in 1787, one finally agreed to after sometimes acrimonious discussions and much compromising of differences. Unfortunately, there were flaws, and the worst was so positioned that it made the rectification of others practically impossible, and it was because of this that informal alterations began to be made and continued to proliferate until they all but submerged the original.

It was not "the people" who literally did the drafting

in Philadelphia, it was delegates designated by the states, but it was special representatives assembled in conventions for that particular purpose who did the ratifying. This is important. Every change since has been ratified by state legislatures, not by such specially chosen conventions. Legislators are elected for other purposes than scrutiny of constitutional amendments, and have only a secondary interest in national affairs. This was what led the Framers to exclude legislatures from the original ratifying process. The principle was carried over into the amending procedure but only if it should be specified by the Congress, and it never has been. No amendment has had the legitimacy of the original.

Ratification of amendments by legislatures was certainly not consistent with the Framers' caution concerning the original Constitution. Why was it allowed? Was it carelessness? Was it done to conciliate the localists among the delegates? Whatever the reason, it was among the most important and least noticed of the Convention's decisions. It made attribution of future amendments to "the people" so unreal as to approach fraud.

19: Contradictions

It is one of the peculiarities of the American situation that not only are there variations of constitutional interpretation but that these variations are strenuously defended and are settled by adversary action. This is to say that fundamental law is, in important respects, shaped by those whose interests and perhaps fortunes are involved.

There is no appeal from the verdict of an impeachment trial no matter how arrived at. No senator has to explain his vote. Whether he agrees with one or another interpretation of the Constitution's words is no one's business but his own. If he is influenced by his estimate of the political consequences it cannot be proved. Preponderance of evidence has no meaning because there is no way of knowing what evidence is relevant. This threatens the end that Madison warned about—that presidents might be found to serve at the pleasure of the Senate.

Or consider the interferences of legislators with executive affairs—intrusions that go under the name of oversight. There is no hint of such powers in the Constitution. They can be enforced, however, by threats of diminished appropriations. About these, legislators have almost unlimited discretion.

Compared with these—and other—powers seized by the legislative branch, neither of the other branches have equal offsetting ones. There is nothing the executive or the judiciary can do that the legislators cannot prevent or stop. Their funds are provided by appropriation. The president's powers are only such as they confer or permit. Even as commander-in-chief his deployment of forces is subject to congressional limitations. (Evasions of this limitation have occurred, but sooner or later they have invariably caused serious repercussions.) Finally, of course, they can impeach any officer of the other branches and drive him from office.

There is complaint that the presidency has become "imperial." It cannot have done so without the active concurrence of the Congress. Its enlargements have followed from recognition that national emergency requires unhindered executive action; emergencies, however, are not defined by the president but by the Congress, and what he may do to meet them is limited by legislative grants. For the same reason—because of its own incapacities—the Congress has created the regulatory agencies. They are justified by the implication that they are necessary to protect the public. They deny altogether the principle of separation. If the Court defines their powers and obligations, it does so with the jurisdictional tolerance of the Congress and they have no responsibility to the president. Their duty is to their creator, but they carry on highly complicated technical operations and are largely self-governing. Their immense bureaucracies constitute a large part of modern government. Their existence is a constant reminder that escape from the Constitution has been accomplished on a grand scale and without notable objection.

Nevertheless, even this massive withdrawal, since it

was authorized by the Congress, can be diminished or abolished by the same body. That body has an even greater power. It can enlarge or diminish its own numbers, define its jurisdiction and control its own budget. It cannot reduce emoluments of the president during his term, or of judges during their service on the bench, but even with these protections, both may still be deprived of office by the legislature and not a few judges have been.

These constitutional realities lead to some peculiar possibilities. Several times the Court has declared legislative acts to be unconstitutional and has on occasion told the president how far his powers extend. It is uncertain what the Court could do if the president refused to comply, saying perhaps that his was an independent branch and not subject to control by another. It is even more startling to contemplate what would happen if the Court declared a law to be unconstitutional and the legislature removed the subject from the Court's jurisdiction and repassed the law.

Judicial supremacy has been approached by the Court in wonderfully discreet fashion, seizing opportunities at rare intervals when rejection of its decrees would be embarrassing to the other branches. The Court seems impregnable, but actually it is wide open to congressional discipline.

Reference has been made to Marshall's dictum concerning the Court's duty to decide whether laws are "conformable to the constitution." He noted further in that same opinion that since judges take an oath to support the Constitution it would be nothing less than immoral to compel them to participate as knowing instruments in the violation of the document they have sworn to support. Concerning this, Pritchett remarks that although "this argument has been ratified by time and by practice" it is still true that the president also takes an oath to support the Constitution and Marshall's own argument would give him the right to refuse enforcement of an act he regards as unconstitutional. Pritchett also finds "equally questionable" the "bland assumption of both Hamilton and Marshall that a judicial finding of repugnance between a statute and the constitution was equivalent to an objective contradiction in the order of nature and not a mere difference of opinion between two guesses."

There may be few who find these arguments convincing, Pritchett continues. "Yet there is a basic uneasiness which will not die, and which occasionally boils up into bitter conflict about the supremacy the supreme court has assumed. . . ."*

The amorphous masses of implication called attention to here, as we have seen, began to appear in the nation's earliest years. An active imagination could visualize a Court powerless to enforce its decrees because it has no agencies for such a purpose except those furnished by an executive it may be proposing to discipline. The same imagination could visualize a legislature passing an act to abolish the recently established "office" of the president, and the president refusing to comply. The treasury is part of his establishment and he might find the funds for its operation without congressional authorization. In emergencies presidents have done things very close to this.

It would be entirely possible for the Congress to reduce the Court to one justice or to provide that its

*C.H. Pritchett, *The American Constitution*, 2nd. ed. (New York: McGraw-Hill, 1968), p. 165.

jurisdiction should not extend to reviewing any legislative act. For a body existing in such a precarious state the Court has been extraordinarily successful in extending its reach even to the legislators who control its existence; still it might at any time be reduced to impotence by a legislative majority.

It has been argued here that the existing quagmire of inference has its cause in the Constitution itself. The separation of powers and concurrent sovereignty, its two basic principles, are not only inconsistent with contemporary governmental responsibility, they were inconsistent with its responsibilities, as we have seen, even in the beginning years. Separation was intended to prevent the lodging of absolute authority in any branch on the assumption that if there was no such lodgment, liberties would be safe. The liberties being protected were for persons and associations outside of government. Everything anyone wanted to do, unless it was criminal, was thus protected.

The Framers' kind of government did not outlast its first years. It soon became necessary for it to do many things its citizens could not do for themselves. Nor could the states do all of them. But the Constitution had not contemplated any such development. Early strict constructionists such as Jefferson thought that even public works were forbidden because they were not specifically authorized and because all residual powers belonged to the states. The refusal of others to agree rested, as we have seen, on the Hamiltonian theory, enunciated when he proposed the national bank. The theory was that if a bank was needed for the government's convenience it could be established simply because the government had first been established.

Jefferson was horrified. But the bank was authorized,

and the strict constructionist's bulwarks were breached. When a state tried to discipline the bank it was prevented from doing so by the Court, resting on its own theory that it must have the power to decide because such a power was inherent in its own creation. This entry on the constitutional scene was not objected to by the Congress, although Marshall is said to have been fearful that it might. It continued to rest on the reasoning of the chief justice, not on amendment.

If Marshall's assumption was "preposterous" as Pritchett remarks, it was no more so than congressional and presidential claims to "privilege." All rested, whatever they might say, on implication, and so none was safely anchored in the Constitution.

20: Return to Legitimacy

The intention in this essay has been to locate and assess early departures from constitutional definition. These, however, when taken together, are so extensive that a conclusion concerning the difficulties of amendment is inevitable. If the original Constitution, as its general neglect demonstrates, has nearly disappeared under the weight of additions, and if it is desirable to have a Constitution, then a careful but complete recasting is indicated. The block to revision must be removed. Beyond that a better method must be adopted for further amendment.

To describe the doubtful legitimacy of many essential activities is admittedly a negative enterprise, helpful only in clearing the way for positive suggestions. The weakness of proposals for comprehensive change is that they will be opposed by formidable interests and actual movement may be checked before it can get under way. The Constitution of 1787 was bitterly opposed too, but there were bold advocates who overcame opposition and departed from constricting terms of reference. Instead of revising the Articles of Confederation as they had been charged to do, the Framers abandoned them and started anew. Such boldness, regarded as admirable in 1787, would be equally admirable at the Constitution's bicentennial.

It has been pointed out that (on June 11) when the question of amendment was discussed in the constitutional convention, George Mason remarked that:

> The plan now to be formed will certainly be defective, as the confederation has been found on trial to be. Amendments therefore will be necessary, and it will be better to provide for them, in an easy, regular constitutional way than to trust to chance and violence.

Madison, in *The Federalist* (48 and 49), also had something to say about revisions. He was expressing concern about keeping the branches from encroaching on each other. His general conclusion was that:

> ... security against a gradual concentration of the several powers in the same department, consists in giving to those who administer each department, the necessary constitutional means, and personal motives, to resist encroachments of the others.

To approach this internal problem he referred, for illustration, to Jefferson's draft of a constitution for Virginia, to be laid before a convention expected to be called in 1783. After acknowledging the respect owed to any suggestion of so "original, comprehensive, and accurate" a thinker, he took leave to dissent from his rather intricate scheme for maintaining the separation of powers. He then came to a general objection, of interest here. This was that although "a constitutional road to a decision of the people, ought to be marked out, and kept open, for certain great and extraordinary occasions..." there appeared to be insuperable objections against the frequent "recurrence to the people."

An objection inherent in the principle was that:

> . . . as every appeal to the people would carry an implication of some defect in the government, frequent appeals would . . . deprive the government of that veneration which time bestows on everything, and without which perhaps the wisest and freest governments would not possess the requisite stability.

This seemed to Madison so important that presently he went on:

> The danger of disturbing the public tranquillity by interesting too strongly the public passions, is a still more serious objection against a frequent reference of constitutional questions, to the decision of the whole society.

There was, however, an even more compelling objection:

> . . . the decisions that would probably result from such appeals, would not answer the purpose of maintaining the constitutional equilibrium.

The legislative branch, he thought, would be most successful in pleading its cause with the people and this would strengthen an already over-strong interest. He concluded that although there were serious objections to "occasional" appeals, "periodical" appeals, were the "proper and adequate means of preventing and correcting infractions of the constitution."

This last he meant to be a warning that departure from the stable balance among the branches would weaken the whole system. This warning continues to be relevant. The piecemeal amendments since Madison's time have for the most part been made with appalling lack of concern for the integrity of the whole. Further revisions ought to be guided by that concern. They ought, in other words, to be undertaken with a clear conception of the contemporary system to be governed by the Constitution.

Solutions for the problems resulting from the doctrine of implication are not to be found in the early departures identified here. These only show that amendment was abandoned almost at once as a means of revision. What is necessary is to say how additions and revisions may be made in ways more appropriate to democracy at the times when they are most needed. The conditions are manifest. Circumstances dictate changes and will not be denied. The procedures for recognizing and acknowledging them ought to be adequate and prompt. Formulations for accommodation ought to be made with care at appropriate periods, and ratification with all deliberate speed ought to be provided for. These conditions require continuing scrutiny by a national body whose qualifications should approximate that of the original Framers.

In a nation grown so large and so complex, improvisations at times of political excitement are more likely to result—as they have—in additions or deletions whose effect on the whole is mischievous. The web of government, touched anywhere, trembles to its very center. Revisionary procedures ought to take careful account of likely consequences, however remote. Such appraisals simply do not happen in crises or in attempts to solve particular problems.

Consider, for instance, the seventeenth amendment providing for the direct election of senators rather than their election by state legislatures. This was intended as a democratizing move but it did not reach the most important consequence of the compromise at the original Convention. Senators should have been freed of their state constituencies. If there is a defense for a second house it must be that it provides a closer look at legislation as it affects the national interest. What the Senate mostly furnishes is a closer look at the impact of proposed legislation on the interests represented by the senators, and these are often adverse to those of the people as a whole.

Neither legislative body has a duty to further national interests. The senatorial amendment conformed to the conception dominant at the Convention of 1787—that adding together the interests of many localities would result in the good of the Union. This theory was in accord with the economics of Adam Smith, so well known in the late eighteenth century and so influential with the Framers. It became obsolete and dangerous when the nation became a complicated but close-coupled system, all of whose citizens saw or read the same news every day, whose localities were hours, not weeks or months, away from each other, whose products were consumed in common, and whose problems, consequently, were national and international far more than local. The Senate could be a general considering body; as constituted it is not required to be by its origins or by the contemporary rewards its members get from their constituents.

Again, consider the twenty-second amendment, limiting presidents to two terms. It was adopted in reaction to Roosevelt's long incumbency, so annoying to all those of conservative instincts who disliked the consequences of his equalitarian policies. These they regarded as disturbances they would rather not have had happen—such, for instance, as the legitimizing of collective bargaining and the institutionalizing of social security. It was feared that a permanent coalition of liberals might perpetuate itself. Limitation on incumbency would at least prevent future presidents from going on and on in office because they offered more and more gifts from the government to masses of voters.

The amendment weakened presidents during the whole of their second terms. This affected among other things their ability to act as party leaders, as proposers of legislation, and as the originators of long-run policies. All of these effects were involved in the change. At the least, political parties should have been strengthened by giving them legality and making them responsible for the sponsorship of national policies; the Congress ought to have had a long-needed reorganization—say, by abandoning the malapportioned Senate and devising a new one with national instead of state origins and affiliations. There could then be a system of assessment looking to the future instead of reacting to crises, and the adoption of an appraisal system would have brought expenditures within expected income thus helping avoid chronic overcommitments.

Roosevelt was not the first president to ignore the tradition of two terms; he was only the first to succeed. Grant was proposed for a third term and came close to accepting. Theodore Roosevelt regretted giving way to Taft and tried to remedy the mistake. True, eight years has usually been enough to suffer many of the mediocre presidents, but when there was merely an unspoken tradition of two terms there was always the possibility of a third and this served a useful political purpose. It enforced some discipline and furnished some continuing political leadership. Since the ratification of the amendment the disintegration of the parties has made them almost useless except for nominating candidates. There is no party policy and no discernible loyalty. They practically disappear for three years after each election.

These are illustrations of what happens when the government as a system is interfered with by amendment for extraneous purposes—in the case of the twenty-second, pure resentment—without considering the whole. But amendments have been few and alterations by implication have been frequent; consequently they offer the most serious instances. Consider, for example, the erection of a shaky structure on the equal protection clause of the fourteenth amendment or the decision that another clause turns corporations into persons. Still more serious, there are the implications drawn from the original Constitution, called attention to in this essay: executive budgeting; congressional oversight of the executive; presidential monopolizing of legislative initiative; the invention of "emergency" and its uses for expanding the powers of the commander-in-chief; the establishment by the Court of judicial supremacy; the strained meaning of concurrent sovereignty—all these and more. There should be added, as well, the use made of the vagueness inherent in many provisions of the Bill of Rights.

By now the government rests on far too thin a constitutional base. That base needs thorough—not piecemeal—reconsideration. It is impossible to be a strict constructionist, and it would be impossible even if the Constitution were satisfactorily reconstituted. There would still be need for future accommodations. Any means used for adaptation to change would be slow and circumstances might require dispatch. It has been noted that even Madison, when he was Jefferson's faithful coworker, admitted that extension could not be avoided, saying, it will be recalled, that they must be guided by "fair and safe rules." Since *fair* and *safe* are words as adaptable to expansion and interpretation as any original clause in the Constitution, it might have been expected that they would have been the center of theoretical exploration to mark the boundaries of implication, but it has not happened. What can be said with some assurance is that fairness and safety can only be reached by fair and safe methods. It is difficult to see how these could be ensured unless through entrustment to agencies created for the purpose. That would not be a court for the trial of adversary actions. It must be other sets of framers, other conventions, and other referenda (or conventions of specially chosen delegates). That may be as close as a democracy can come to an approximation of what is fair and safe.

The effort of those concerned ought not to be the preservation of a Constitution but the restoration of constitutionality.

Index